PRINCE

Published in 2021 by Welbeck
An Imprint of Welbeck Non-Fiction Limited,
part of Welbeck Publishing Group
20 Mortimer Street London W1T 3JW

A CIP catalogue record for this book is available from
the British Library

ISBN 978 1 78739 164 2

10 9 8 7 6 5 4 3 2 1

Printed in Dubai

PRINCE

A PORTRAIT OF THE ARTIST IN MEMORIES & MEMORABILIA

PAUL SEXTON

WELBECK

CONTENTS

Opposite: Prince poses in the Netherlands in 1981.

FOREWORD

BY SUSAN ROGERS

A couple of days after Prince passed away unexpectedly in 2016, many of us who knew him felt an immediate pull to gather together in Minneapolis, the place where he had first brought us so many years ago. About 40 of us – from Prince's youth to his recent crew – huddled in a cocktail lounge at the Loews Minneapolis Hotel across from the famous First Avenue nightclub downtown. Wendy Melvoin of the Revolution had the foresight to set up a microphone and Matt Larson from the 1980s-era tech crew ran it through a small sound system. The hotel had given us the lounge to use all to ourselves that night. So we did. One after another we took the mic and told Prince stories.

Alan Leeds told of pushing a mattress down a hallway in a deluxe Parisian hotel at 2 o'clock in the morning and Susannah Melvoin told a hilarious story of snorkeling in the Mediterranean with Prince where he pulled a string of unprecedented (for Prince) moves out of his virtual hat and made her laugh so hard underwater that she was afraid she'd drown. Matt Larson told of how, on the Purple Rain tour, an exhausted Prince had signaled Matt over to him between songs and called for "the oxygen!" Matt showed up with guitar tech Rick Garcia, thinking that he heard Prince call for the Mexican. Prince's effort to catch his breath was made worse for laughter. Lisa Coleman told of their very first meeting, the awkward silence in the car as he drove her from the airport to his home, and how two of the quietest people in the world ultimately communicated by playing piano for each other. Mark Brown told of being 18-years-old and working as a short-order cook in a pancake house when Prince dropped in late one night to invite him to join the Revolution and tour the world. Poignantly, Mayte told of knowing him as his fan, his dancer, his wife, and the mother of his only child.

The funniest was Robbie Pastor's hysterical story of the terror he felt in his role as the "advance man" for a Prince visit to London. Robbie arrived just hours before his boss and saw that the hotel had misunderstood his instructions. Instead of the requested grand piano in Prince's suite, there was an electronic keyboard and a little amp. Robbie remembered standing on the balcony of an ancient London hotel, cigarette smoke and sweat in his eyes, guiding a baby grand piano being lowered by a crane into the top floor suite where a waiting piano tuner might, if all of the stars were aligned, get it tuned before Prince walked in the door from Heathrow airport. They made it in the nick of time! Prince, unaware of the heroic efforts and gargantuan cost spent in the previous hours on his behalf, walked into the suite, dropped his bag at the piano, sat down and played.

It is a tribute to Prince's life that so many of these stories were so funny. On that sad, sad night, sharing our stories made us laugh with amusement and amazement at what life in his orbit was like. It was a reminder of the powerful gravitational pull that he had on all who were close to him. Most of those stories had the common theme of how hard we worked for him and how his own excellence was enough to bring out the best in us. We in that room knew him, and so we knew that in this closed circle, there wasn't any need to explain, describe, defend, or promote him; we could just tell what happened. We shared what we loved about him and what had astonished us the most. There was no shortage of material. We talked long into the night, wiping away tears of sorrow and joy. I remember thinking, "This is what every Prince fan should know. THIS is the story."

Only by collecting stories across all of the dimensions of this enigmatic man's life will he be known in the same way that people close to him knew him. During his lifetime, Prince carefully controlled how much of himself he was willing to let the public know. That kind of privacy was necessary so that all of his drive for self-expression could be funneled into his lyrics and, sometimes, his movies. Now that he is gone, private moments from Prince's life spent with friends, musicians, collaborators and staff – those stories that comprised one remarkable man's tale – can be told.

I am pleased to write that Paul Sexton has begun this endeavor by asking people who knew Prince to share their memories, and by presenting them to readers unadorned and unfiltered. This book does not focus on Prince's music, his methods, his history or his influence on culture or on other musicians. It lets the people who knew and worked with him tell our stories so that readers can get to know a little better the man whose singular talent and prodigious creative output is unlikely to be equaled any time soon. When the individual stories of his life emerge like pixels on a screen, the public image of Prince will get closer and closer to the truth of who he was. Just as it is with the greatest mysteries of the natural world, knowing more about Prince does nothing to lessen the wonder we feel when we think about what he accomplished; it only deepens our appreciation. Even the most mythic stories can be told in plain language.

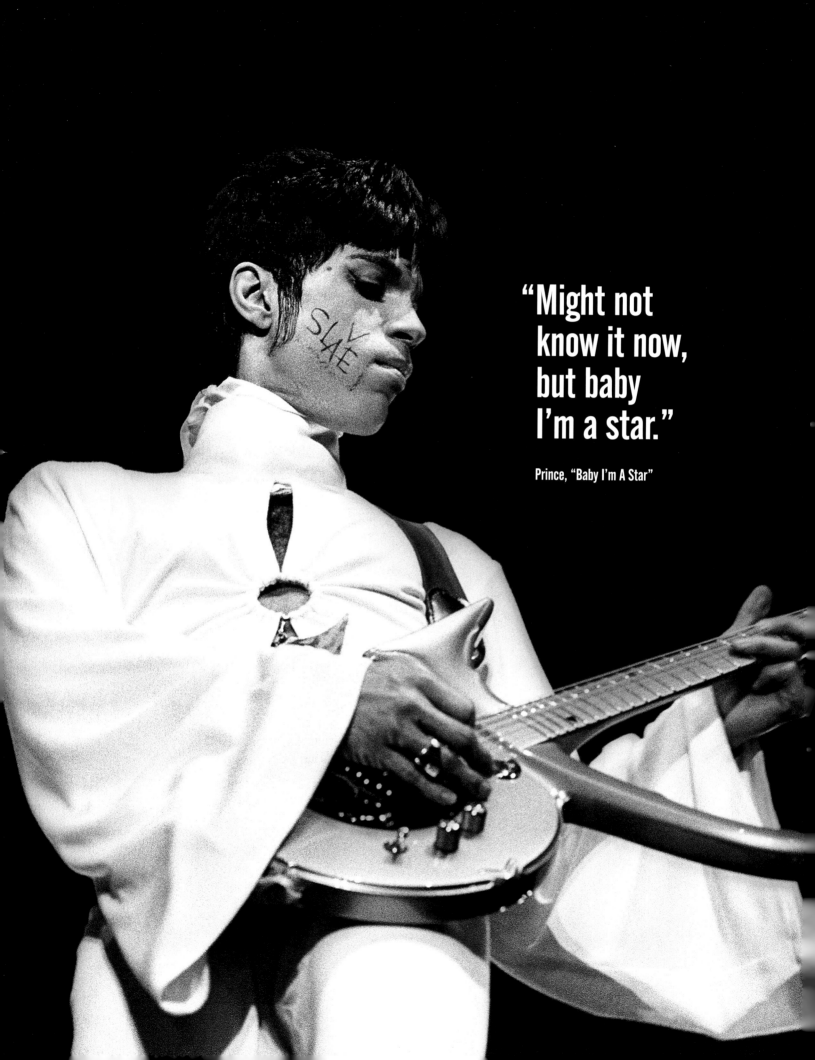

"Might not
know it now,
but baby
I'm a star."

Prince, "Baby I'm A Star"

INTRODUCTION

THE BEAUTIFUL ONE

Far more willingly than we approached any school lesson, we grew up learning the fundamental hierarchy of music. Elvis was always The King. Aretha was the Queen of Soul, the Temptations its Emperors, Nina Simone its High Priestess. Elton became Captain Fantastic, and The Beatles were just The Beatles. Such was their dominion, they didn't even need a designation. Even when you couldn't always apply yourself to learning about actual royal bloodlines and heads of church and state, those titles stuck fast.

Accession to such a sacrosanct social order was rare indeed, but in the latter part of the 1970s, suddenly there was someone who seemed to arrive fully-formed and magnificent from the get-go. He was, in one literal sense, born a Prince, and from the first time we clapped ears on him, every soul boy and girl was under his spell. In the era just before MTV took the wheel, and while Prince's early releases remained inexplicably specialist in the UK, it was a while before British audiences truly saw him. When we did, it was all over.

This volume doesn't expect to trace every contour of Prince Rogers Nelson's life and influence. It hopes instead to provide both the passionate devotee and the passing friend with a series of first-hand appreciations, not from mere armchair admirers but those whose lives Prince touched. In some cases, although he may not always have shown it as fulsomely as they might have liked, these are the memories of those who touched him, fraternally, creatively, spiritually and romantically.

I was fortunate to win the collaborative trust of many of this holy order of insiders when, after his shocking death, I made the deep-dive documentary 'Prince And Me' for BBC Radio 2. My thanks go to that fraternity for sharing stories about the man they knew – their boss, inspiration and taskmaster, a man who expected perfection of himself and, therefore, of all those he invited in. So dig, if you will, the picture of a singular human, flawed and fragile like all of us, but fizzing with playful, dangerous energy like a firecracker in a phone booth. I'm grateful for the particularly tireless support and enthusiasm of Susan Rogers, both for the vivid pictures she paints in the narrative and for her eloquent and elegant foreword. The image of that distinguished band of brothers and sisters, bound together by an unforgettable enigma and sitting together, soon after he departed, to trade often hilarious anecdotes, will live long. So will Prince, because like only the very best of the best that we have lost too soon, he's still with us and always will be.

Paul Sexton
May 2021

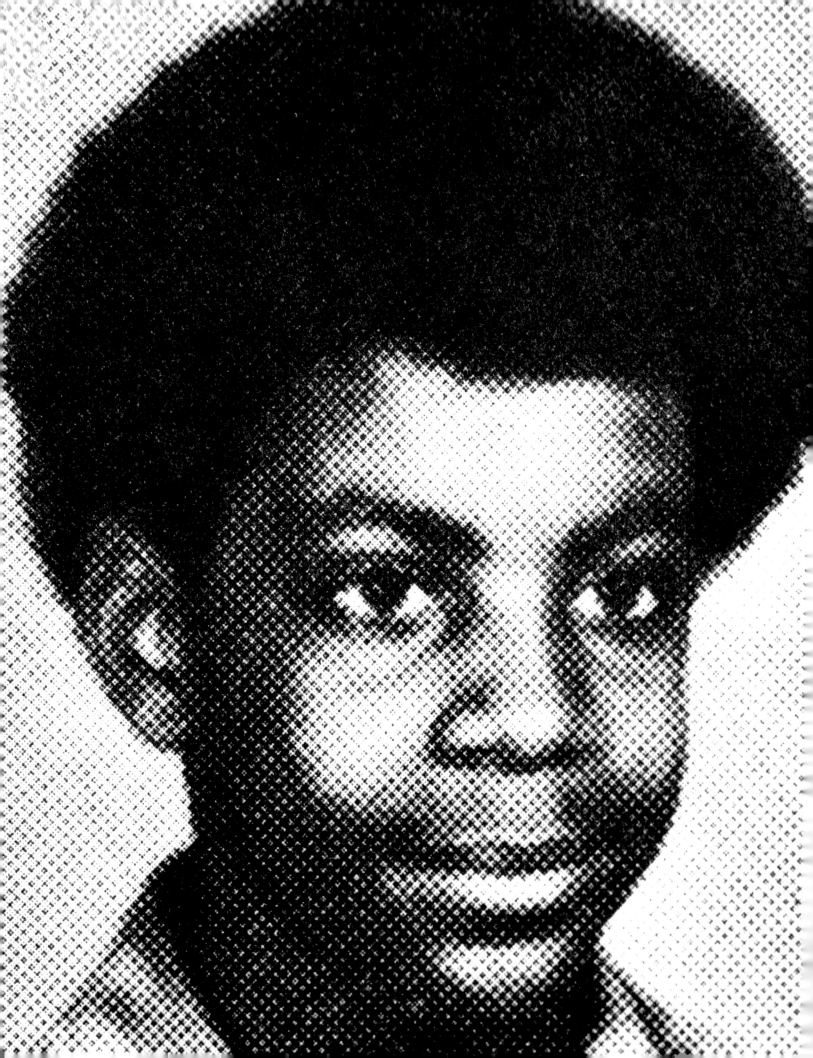

CHAPTER ONE

THE PRE-TEEN PRINCE

Previous page: With "slave" on his cheek, Prince plays Brabanthallen, Den Bosch, Netherlands, in March 1995, on the tour named – with typically confident finesse – The Ultimate Live Experience.

Opposite: The young Prince Rogers Nelson sits for an eighth grade class picture. The son of musician John Nelson and singer Mattie Shaw was already well-versed in music, having written his first song at the age of seven.

It's the late summer of 1970, and a young man called André Anderson is getting acclimatized. The youngest of six, he's been growing up in challenging circumstances, as his mother Bernadette, a social worker and community leader, works hard to make ends meet in a poor area of Minneapolis. Bernadette had fallen pregnant with André's oldest brother when she was just 14.

But now she is recently divorced from her husband, musician Fred, who had disapproved of Bernadette's ambitions to get an education and to strive for a better life for herself and her children. She seizes her new opportunities and moves the family across town. In years to come, her youngest will carve a name for himself as André Cymone. But at this point, he's just the new kid in school, where he makes the new friend who will help to reroute his life.

"I grew up in a different part of north Minneapolis," Cymone told me, eloquently surveying his youth. "My family moved from where we lived, my mother was able to get a better job and got us into a different community. She got me out of a lifestyle that wasn't … you know, all that conducive. So I went to a new school and a new situation."

Many of us remember that uneasy playground feeling of being among complete strangers and disapproving stares. Everyone seems to know everyone, except for you; and you wouldn't mind if the ground opened up so you could disappear. But, on that dreaded first day at Lincoln Junior High School, 2131 Twelfth Avenue North, André is about to find a kindred spirit.

"I remember the first day of school," he said. "The gym teacher, or whoever he was, he gives you your programme for you to go through your classes. He gives that to me and says, 'Go and stand against the wall.' I look down this wall of all these people and I don't know

anybody. Everybody looked, like, 'Don't stand here.' It was really kind of strange.

"So I looked down the row and I saw this one kid, and he reminded me a little bit of myself. I thought, 'I'm going to go and stand next to him.' So I started talking to him and saying, 'How you doing? I'm André.' He said, 'I'm Prince.'"

Prince Rogers Nelson is also from a broken home and similarly separated from a musician father. Born on June 7, 1958, his very name is his father John's stage identity, in his guise as pianist and leader of the Prince Rogers Trio. The youngster's life map is sketched early: he's a mere five years old when he sees John perform. Watching the audience's reaction had a profound and lasting effect. He later acknowleged this as a pivotal moment in his musical development.

John Nelson had moved to Minneapolis in the early 1950s and, in the middle of the decade, married the singer Mattie Shaw. They met at one of the trio's performances, at Minneapolis's Phyllis Wheatley House, and he recruited her to sing with them. When their son was just seven, he wrote his first song, 'Funk Machine', on his dad's piano, which he learned to play by ear.

Prince taught himself by practising the TV themes of his childhood, such as *The Man from U.N.C.L.E.* and (ironically, since it would re-enter his life much later) *Batman*. His sister Tyka, two years his junior,

> **"There were two Princes in the house where we lived. The older one with all the responsibilities of heading a household and the younger one whose only *modus operandi* was fun."**
>
> **Prince, The Beautiful Ones**

was his audience. Even his 'Funk Machine' title was ahead of its time. This was 1965, when even the Godfather of Soul, James Brown, was only in the formative stages of honing the immortal groove that the word "funk" would come to represent.

"There were two Princes in the house where we lived," Prince recalled in his memoir *The Beautiful Ones,* which he was writing at the time of his death in 2016. "The older one with all the responsibilities of heading a household and the younger one whose only *modus operandi* was fun."

On the admirably opulent prince.com official website, his multi-media biography recalls his autobiographical *Piano and a Microphone* concert at Paisley Park, performed three months before his death. There, Prince re-enacted being enchanted by the sight of John's piano, when he was a mere three years old. "Here comes dad," he remembered. "I'm not supposed to touch his piano, but I want to play it so bad."

Prince's parents separated when he was seven. They divorced when he was ten, after which Mattie married Heyward Baker. A few years after that her maverick son started running away. The first time he left the family home at 2620 Eighth Avenue North, it was after clashing with his stepfather.

He missed his father, who left behind a piano, and briefly went to

live with him downtown. Although this apartment would become just one of a long list of addresses the young Prince would stay in around the city, the time he spent at John's strengthened the musical bond that would later see them write together. He would go on to call John his best friend.

Prince told *Musician* magazine: "He told me one time that he has dreams where he'd see a keyboard in front of his eyes, and he'd see his hands on the keyboard and he'd hear a melody. And he can get up and it can be like 4.30 a.m. and he can walk right downstairs to his piano and play the melody."

Wayfaring around his hometown did little to make Prince love it. "Have you ever been to Minneapolis?" he asked a reporter from the Night Owl entertainment section of New Jersey's *The Aquarian Weekly.* "It's a really small joint and if you really dig country & western music, that's the place to go.

"The radio stations don't play any new wave music, they only play country & western music," he went on. "The clothes, the dance,

Opposite: Prince poses with teammates for an eighth grade basketball game.

Above: By his sophomore year, Prince was immersed in the inspiration of funk, soul and rock from far and wide.

the music, everything is so behind. I'd call my sister, who lives [in Manhattan] and ask her what was going on. I was shocked because we got everything she talked about six months later."

So now, here he was on that momentous school day with his fellow new boy, feeling a rare sense of connection. The future André Cymone resumes the story, and remembers how he reacted to hearing that unusual first name. "I said, 'Cool, what are you into?' and he said, 'I'm into music.' I said, 'Oh wow, so am I.' I said, 'What do you play?' 'Piano, guitar, what do you play?' 'Bass, drums, horns.' He said, 'We should go and jam.' So basically we started talking. That's the first time we met."

The friendship between the Nelson kid and the Anderson boy grew quickly. "He invited me over to his dad's house," said André, "and said, 'My dad has a little set-up. We can hang out and jam.' It was the first person I ever met that, as we were talking, had the same attitude that I had. I was a very outspoken person, so it was strange to meet someone who seemed to be in that state of mind. Literally nobody else where I came from even came close.

"People got tired of me always telling them that one day I was going to do this or do that. I was this good, I was that good. Most of the people would laugh at me and say, 'Yeah, sure. You're never going to get off the city block.' He was the first person I ever met that actually had that same kind of attitude. It became our bonding point."

On prince.com, Cymone says: "He sat at his father's piano and played several television and movie theme songs. I played along on a large-scale ukulele. I think for the first time in his life – and I know for the first time in mine – we found someone in each other who took music and all its possibilities extremely seriously. I think, after that day, we were pretty much inseparable. We hung out all the time."

The name would, of course, be a point of conversation. "He looked at me with that look that I got to know a whole lot better," Cymone told me, "because I said, 'There's a dog at the end of our block named Prince.' He looked at me, like, 'That's messed up, man'. I wasn't lying.

It was a little Scottish terrier, and it was the only [other] thing I've ever known named Prince. But I told him, "That's actually a really cool name."

In 1980, Prince told the *Los Angeles Times*: "I think my father was kind of lashing out at my mother when he named me Prince. We were never an immediate family. When I was 12, I ran away for the first time because of problems with my stepfather. I went to live with my real father but that didn't last too long because he's as stubborn as I am. I lived with my aunt for a while. I was constantly running from family to family."

The more Cymone shared with me about his new friend of those days, the more it became clear that, even in adolescence, Prince was a distinctive human being, wise beyond his years. Perhaps it was his diminutive, 5' 2" stature, even as an adult, that first prompted him to see off hostility with intelligence wherever possible. But his insightful advice certainly diffused one early flashpoint.

"I was the youngest of six, and my older brothers were very rough," André said. "So I wasn't going to have a whole lot of time for people saying anything that I didn't like. Prince was telling me about this one kid who was going to talk about me and my family. He was saying, 'This is what you've got to do.'

"He had this notebook, and it was full of stuff. He said, 'This is what you say about him,' and he had the names of this guy's mom and dad and brothers. He said 'His mom's name is Birdie, and his dad's name is Herman.' He had all this information. He said 'When he starts talking about your family …' I'd just met him, and he's going through this whole thing. I said 'Why can't I just punch him?'

"He said, 'If you punch him, you're going to have to punch his brother, and his other brother, and he's got a whole bunch of cousins …' At that moment, I thought, this dude is really cool. I just met this guy and he's trying to give me a breakdown on how to deal with people. He was just showing me the ropes of the neighborhood and the lay of the land.

"I'm like a bull in a china shop. Say something about me, we're going to have a problem. But he was trying to get me to avoid all that. It became a common thread between us," said Cymone, "and we became friends before we really got as deep into the music as we got."

With Prince's domestic issues, soon he sensed a solution. He asked André whether he could move in. When he asked, his friend knew he

Right: Feeling the funk. Prince performs with André Cymone (left) and Dez Dickerson (right) during the Dirty Mind Tour of 1981.

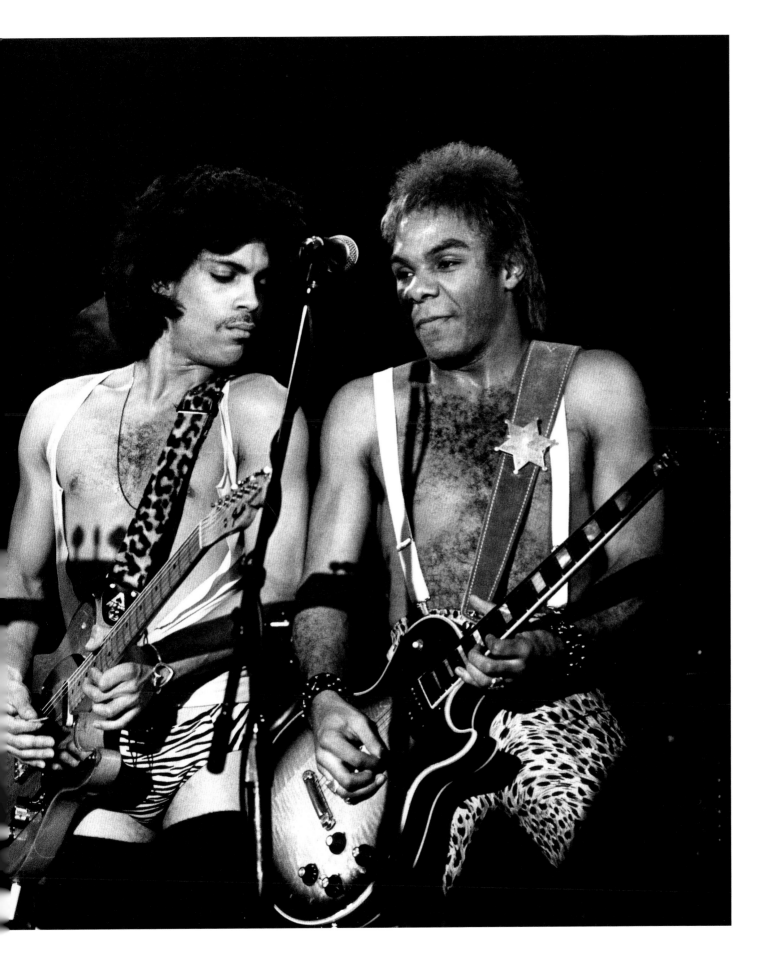

would need permission. "I said, 'Man, you got to ask my mom. It's great with me.' My older brothers were into their thing, so to have somebody my age living at the crib, I thought that would be great.

"So he went and talked to my mom, and she was like 'I'm going to have to talk to *your* mom. I can't just have you run away and live here.' So she talked to his mom and they worked it out. He came and lived with us, originally in the same room." The family home was at 1244 Russell Ave N., in the Near North district of Minneapolis.

Cymone's mother, Bernadette, was a force for good in Prince's life. The obsessive work ethic that we will learn about later can be traced back in part to "Queen Bernie," so much so that she rated a namecheck in a track from 1992's *Love Symbol* album, 'The Sacrifice Of Victor'.

"My mother's main demand and his main responsibility," André says on the website, "was to help around the house and make it to school on time and maintain good grades. I think that was it, and he did that."

Then came the realization that you don't know how you *really* feel about someone until you live with them. Especially when you're cooped up in the same room. "Originally, we didn't get along at all," said Cymone to me with a laugh. "I always had to sleep with music, he always had to sleep with music, and our music tastes would vary drastically.

Opposite: Prince and Canadian bassist Rhonda Smith at the 2013 *Billboard* Music Awards. Smith toured and recorded with Prince for nearly ten years. "From the outset he schooled me on a lot of music," she said.

Above: A fan pays a simple, heartfelt tribute to Prince outside Cymone's family home in North Minneapolis. After bouncing between homes as a teenager, he found some stability there.

"So to be in the same room, we had to choose. We'd either flip a coin, or say 'You chose last night.' He might pick Seals and Crofts, I might pick Earth, Wind & Fire. He might pick Blood, Sweat & Tears or Chicago. But it just got to a point where the room was too small. I literally had to make a line. It doesn't really make me look good, but it is what it is."

It was a fascinating time capsule to hear Cymone talking about their respective favourites of the day. Prince's love for the funk heroes of the early 1970s such as Sly and the Family Stone and, later, Graham Central Station (formed by ex-Sly bassist Larry Graham) is widely discussed and debated.

A more infrequent, but quite logical, thread is his admiration for Blood, Sweat & Tears, the American band fronted by the soulful voice of Canadian David Clayton-Thomas. Or, indeed, his predilection for the superior soft-rock of singer-songwriters Seals and Crofts, who released a series of gold and platinum-selling albums in the US in the first half of the decade.

He would frequently pass on his accumulated learning to those that played with him. Canadian bassist Rhonda Smith, who recorded and toured with Prince for nearly ten years, told *Bass Player* magazine in 2004: "From the outset he schooled me on a lot of music – guys like Larry Graham, James Jamerson, Willie Weeks and Chuck Rainey.

"Plus, he's a phenomenal bassist – he plays from the heart," Smith explained. "If he wants you to reproduce a feel, he comes over and plays it for you, so you need to be able to do it on the spot, which is not easy." But on disc, he would frequently just do the job himself.

"He knows what he wants and he can play it, so why not?" she said. "If it's 3am and he's in the studio alone, he's going to put down the bass track himself, even though the band is on call whenever he wants to record."

Above: Master P. Nelson is captured for the high school yearbook.
Opposite: The barrier-breaking, genre-bending Sly & The Family Stone were early and enduring influences on Prince's songwriting.

Prince's later engineer Susan Rogers would tell me: "He was well-schooled in music by the time he got his first record deal. That's a lesson that shouldn't be lost on the young people of today. If you're going to be great at something, you have to study the history of the art that came before you."

He would soon be downplaying the role of outside influences in his work. "If I listen to a record, I hear something that I'd like to do differently, and I become too critical of it," Prince told the *Twin Cities Reader* in 1979. "You shouldn't be that way, because the group took their time and effort and worked on it. I'd rather just do my own thing."

But back in those cramped Minneapolis quarters … "His side was always neat, he was a lot more organized," remembered André. "My side was absolute mayhem. I had girls' numbers written on the wall, I had my trumpet, and it was actually bunk beds. Then we separated them and put them on both sides of the room. Even that didn't work. Prince said, 'Can I go and stay down in the basement?' and my mom said yes, that was cool.

"His dad would let him use his organ every now and again, but

when we started off, he didn't have his own guitar, and I didn't have my own bass. So he just had that keyboard that his dad would let him use from time to time.

"He was always prolific. I was upstairs, he was downstairs, he would write something and come up and say 'You got to hear this.' He'd play it to me, and I'd write something and say 'You got to hear this,' and we'd go back and forth. It really became a very competitive kind of thing, like 'How many songs did you write?' 'I wrote four, how many did you write?' 'I wrote six.' That's what we did. That was our fun, that was our space."

In the autumn of 1983, as a young reporter for the British pop weekly *Record Mirror*, I had interviewed Cymone. This was at the time of his solo US soul chart entry 'Make Me Wanna Dance' and, back then, he was even more descriptive about their cohabiting arrangements.

"We grew up in the same house – the same bedroom, actually, if you want to talk about areas," he said. "He didn't get along with his parents too well and I didn't either, I was kind of the black sheep. I was into women and driving cars that didn't belong to me. His parents knew about that and didn't want him to be around me.

"So he stayed with me, but it didn't really work out too well," explained André, "'cos I'm pretty wild and when I met him, he didn't even cuss. He came into a totally different environment – my family are pretty open, but we carried it a bit too far." They did things, I wrote at the time, that would make your hair blush. "We had a lot of girls round at the house and often they didn't have many clothes on."

In 1981, as Prince began to withdraw regular media access for interviews, he reminisced about those days to *Rolling Stone*. "I grew up on the borderline. I had a bunch of white friends, and I had a bunch of black friends. I never grew up in any one particular culture. I took a lot of heat all the time. People would say something about our clothes or the way we looked or who we were with, and we'd end up fighting."

So much for his advice about turning the other cheek.

Back in that basement, years of jamming would ensue. The pair would often skip school early, along with André's sister Linda and other like minds, rehearsing themselves into shape to create the band Grand Central. "When I went to jam over at his father's house, this is how I found out that this dude was really good," said Cymone.

"His dad had this really deep voice, he was like 'Hey, Skipper'. Prince's nickname was Skipper, all his family called him that. One of the first things I said to him was 'You actually let people call you Skipper?'

"Anyway, his dad comes in, he's looking at me and he says 'Who's this?' and Prince says 'Dad, this is André.' And he's looking at me like I'm suspect. I go over to the piano and I say, 'Excuse me, but who is that?' And I point to the picture of my dad. And he looks at the picture and he looks at me, and he does this a few times and then he busts out in this big, deep laugh.

"Me and Prince are looking at each other thinking, 'What's so funny?' and he goes 'You're Fred Anderson's son! Oh my god!' and he's bending backwards laughing. I'm like 'OK, what's the joke?' He says 'You boys

Magic contained here … Prince's first
reel-to-reel demo tape, recorded in
1977 when he was 18 years old.

SOUND80

PRINCE

7½ IPS ¼ Track

1. Just As Long As We're Together
2. Baby
3. Soft And Wet
4. My Love Is Forever
5. I Hope We Can Work It Out
6. Make It Through The Storm
7. Jelly Jam

© Prince 1977
℗ Prince

All Rights Reserved

used to play together when you was little. Fred was in a band with me, he played bass.' It turns out that, ironically, our dads played together." Thus began the adventure that led, slowly, to Prince's solo record deal with Warner Brothers. But he walked that path with surprising hesitancy, still anxious to be a team player. "We said, 'We should start a band,'" remembered Cymone, "but we didn't really have any instruments. The name of the band eventually became Grand Central, but it started off with a few different names. The next thing was to cut a better demo, so we cut some of my songs and some of Prince's."

Grand Central coalesced around 1974, when Prince was 16. Progress was sedate, and line-ups volatile. Prince's cousin Charles "Chazz" Smith was replaced by Morris Day, later to lead the new star's protégés The Time. But, as Grand Central played local battle-of-the-band nights, a reputation formed as one of the North Side's cooler bands.

Prince eventually gravitated towards his first, three-album solo deal with Warners, insisting en route that Cymone stay with him and aiming for a Brothers Johnson-style partnership. André did, for a time, playing in the band that Prince formed after his Warners debut.

But he soon wanted to gain his own wings. "He's into raunchy sex and I'm into technology," Cymone told me candidly in 1983. "Eventually I said 'If I stay now, I'll be doing this the rest of my life.'" But two years later, he had his biggest solo success when his recording of Prince's song 'The Dance Electric' made the American R&B Top 10.

This volume deliberately looks to sidestep the full-fat, well-worn biographical treatment of its hero, but it's irresistible to share what may have been his first-ever press cutting, from his high school journal. In a story in the student newspaper the *Central High Pioneer* from February 1976, when he was in his senior year, the would-be artist told Lisa Crawford about his struggles, in a piece headlined "Nelson Finds It 'Hard To Become Known'."

"I was born here, unfortunately," he said of his Minneapolis background. "I think it is very hard for a band to make it in this state, even if they're good. Mainly because there aren't any big record companies or studios in this state. I really feel that if we would have lived in Los Angeles or New York or some other big city, we would have gotten over by now."

The story namechecked Prince's music teacher, Mr Bickham, and his predecessor, Mrs Doepkes, whom he praised for letting him work on his own. The teenager was, by now, playing guitar, bass, drums and keyboards, but regretted that he had not kept up his studies on the saxophone.

"I've had about two lessons, but they didn't help much," he said. "I think you'll always be able to do what your ear tells you, so just think how great you'd be with lessons also," he said. "I advise anyone who wants to learn guitar to get a teacher unless they are very musically inclined. One should learn all their scales too. That is very important." Such were the early days of a smart young man with funk in his very DNA.

> ## "I've had about two lessons, but they didn't help much."
> Prince, 1976

CHAPTER TWO

BABY I'M A STAR:

PRINCE, THE FIRST TIME

Opposite: Photographed for the *Minneapolis Tribune* in 1978, Prince, 19, was primed for stardom. "I don't like categories at all," he told the newspaper.

A career that travels across five decades will stop to take new passengers on board at every release; and we all have our cherished memories of the first time Prince came into our lives. Some of us did it from afar, others at closer quarters that would, further down the line, turn us from fans into trusted confederates.

My own journalistic timeline as an archetypal cub reporter began a few months before Prince made his recording debut with the self-created Warner Bros album *For You* in the spring of 1978. This was an almost forgotten time in British pop culture when the weekly music press held sway. Daily newspapers were still some years away from committing to dedicated pop coverage, and the *NME*, *Sounds*, *Melody Maker* and *Record Mirror* could between them claim actual sales of about 700,000 copies. Modern marketing executives would pay a pretty price for that many eyeballs, in today's parlance.

My freelance path as a teenage *Record Mirror* correspondent, one of many, soon took me toward the all-pervading disco soul boom of the day. But not, at first, to Prince. As with much of his early work, the British profile of that first album was modest. The same went for its subsequent singles 'Soft and Wet' (a title that, unsurprisingly, made many late-70s radio programmers distinctly nervous) and 'Just as Long as We're Together'. But then that profile was mixed even back in the USA, with the latter song an R&B hit but neither single up to much in the pop crossover stakes. Prince did have his UK advocates, such as the prominent DJ Chris Hill, who spun 'Just as Long as We're Together' as it flickered on to *Record Mirror*'s UK Disco Top 90.

It's almost impossible to imagine a day when Prince was not a name in every household. But a search for the very earliest media mentions of the star of our story revealed an entertaining discovery in the pages of *Billboard*. In January 1978, as he continued work on that *For You* debut, in which he jumped between 27 instruments, the magazine reported in its Studio Track column that, at the Record Plant studio in Los Angeles, "Warner Bros *group* Prince" were tracking, with executive producer Tommy Vicari at the board.

A band indeed. And *Billboard* wasn't alone. Back in 1976, when the 18-year-old Prince *was* still in a band, he helped early champion Chris Moon make a demo for his Moon Sound Studio in south Minneapolis. The teenage prodigy added piano to it, then bass, drums, electric guitar and backing vocals. Moon played the newly augmented tape to an industry friend. "Not bad," he said. "Who are they?"

With *For You*, Prince became the youngest artist to produce an entire LP in Warner Bros' history. "I thought I knew my material better than any other producer and it seemed like I was best suited for the job," he told *Right On!* magazine, matter-of-fact as could be.

Then, to the *Minneapolis Tribune* on the record's release: "I don't like categories at all. I'm not soul and I'm not jazz, but everyone wants to call me one or the other. The Bee Gees aren't called soul," he said (at the time the Gibb brothers were at the height of their all-conquering reign). "They're pop or something. Whatever it is to whoever is listening to it, it is what it is."

Another early interview, with *Insider* magazine, appeared just after

the debut single 'Soft and Wet' had started to get airplay in the early summer of 1978. "I was driving down the street in my Datsun the first time I heard it," Prince said. "It wasn't that I couldn't believe it, it's simply that my heart dropped to my knees."

By the autumn of 1978, *Billboard* had realized that, for all his prodigious, multi-instrumental skills, Prince was nevertheless a solo act. A one-liner reported that he had personally attended the evening festivities of Warner Communications' WEA Records trade gathering. He was there with Chaka Khan, whose *Chaka* album featuring 'I'm Every Woman' was about to appear, the country rock band Firefall and Fleetwood Mac's Stevie Nicks.

It was in the second half of 1979 that a bohemian 21-year-old made himself heard in the UK with a sound we couldn't miss: the voluptuously infectious 'I Wanna Be Your Lover'. From the sophomore *Prince* album, which he created in just six weeks, the track scaled *Billboard*'s R&B chart to seize the reins from the Commodores' 'Still' in December. That Motown entry was the only ballad chart-topper in an era that gave us such individualistic statements – of which Prince would have approved – as Funkadelic's '(Not Just) Knee Deep' and Rufus & Chaka Khan's 'Do You Love What You Feel'.

Living in south London, I recall the superior grooves of 'I Wanna Be Your Lover' blasting into the 'burbs from Capital Radio. I specifically remember its debut on the station's London chart, the Capital Countdown, one Saturday morning in January 1980. It was super-smart, the way Chic were at the same time, with just enough of a retro-funk vibe to hook an older crowd but with the confidence to usher in a new decade of music that Prince would come to dominate.

The single scraped into the radio station's London-based Top 30, but just missed the all-important Top 40 on the official, BBC-endorsed national survey. The truth is, we weren't ready. The soul music that was selling in that first month of 1980 had the softest possible focus, be it Billy Preston and Syreeta's 'With You I'm Born Again' or KC and the Sunshine Band's 'Please Don't Go'. Or, as in one case, the R&B sound might be 18 years old, as Booker T and the MGs' 'Green Onions' sprouted in the Top 10. Prince, absurdly, would not be seen on the UK singles chart again for three years.

Three thousand miles away, as 'I Wanna Be Your Lover' took possession of America's R&B airwaves, Susannah Melvoin was among those instantly entranced. Still 15, she and twin sister Wendy and their older brother Jonathan were growing up in a musical milieu fostered by their father, the revered jazz pianist and in-demand studio sideman Mike Melvoin.

Opposite and **Above:** Prince performs at the celebrated Roxy Theater on Sunset Strip, West Hollywood, in 1979.

Wendy would go on to join Prince's band The Revolution with Lisa Coleman and to form their own exceptional duo, Wendy & Lisa. Susannah would later become close to Prince both professionally and personally, and joined an expanded edition of The Revolution. But in 1978, she was a mere superfan.

"The first time I became aware of Prince was when I was in eighth grade," she told me in 2017. "Wendy and I were living in the northern United States, far up in the White Mountains of New Hampshire, just at the border of Maine. Long story short, at night, when it was very cold in the wintertime, and there were no radio frequencies getting in the way of others, we would click into Boston radio.

"One night we heard 'I Wanna Be Your Lover'. We were like,

"One night we heard 'I Wanna Be Your Lover'. We were like, '*Who* is this fantastic female singer?'" Wendy Melvoin

'*Who* is this fantastic female singer?' We literally thought it was a girl, but turned that around quickly. We did our homework, and fell madly in love with this music."

Prince followed up with a second single from his self-titled second album, 'Why You Wanna Treat Me So Bad'. Its January 1980 US release was marked by an appearance on *American Bandstand,* watched at home by his future keyboard player of nearly two decades, the New Power Generation's Morris Hayes.

"I remember watching him, sitting at home," he told Music Feeds. "My mom was watching, too – she was like, 'Ooh! Who's that devil?!' I actually got to tell him that story one time. We were on the road somewhere, just talking. I think he might have said someone or something was 'the Devil', y'know … it clicked in the back of my head. I was like, 'You gotta watch who you call a devil, man! My mom said that about you when you were on *Bandstand*!' My mom eventually found out he was quite the opposite."

Prince was interviewed on that edition by longtime host Dick Clark, which now seems an impossible mash-up of musical generations, as if, say, Ed Sullivan was talking to Lady Gaga. "It was a weird interview he did with Dick, man," said Hayes. "I found out later that he used to get real nervous when he was on TV like that.

"Dick was asking him these questions, and he was gesturing really strangely and actin' all weird. He was shy in that kind of environment; he'd withdraw and be aloof. When he wasn't playing music, he was really something different."

Within a few months of Susannah and Wendy Melvoin falling in love with Prince's music, the man himself would come much closer to their world. "I think it was the following summer that we got a call from Lisa Coleman saying she got this gig," said Susannah, "and she was going out on the road. We were like, 'What kind of gig and where are you going?'

"Now, Lisa and her family were very close with our family. Her father and my father were session players in Los Angeles. They started in New York, came to LA, and it just became that the two families were alike in so many ways. They had three kids, we had three kids, so we all just grew up together.

"Lisa called to tell us she'd got this gig. She said, 'I'm going on the road with Prince,' and we just flipped out. It was the greatest, inspired news. We were just kids, but we were so in love with this music. We were like, 'I can't believe we're getting this close to him because Lisa's got this gig!'"

Susan Rogers' admiration of Prince was perhaps on a more scholarly level. Certainly, the love of A-list soul and funk that they shared helped her get the gig when he was searching for a sound engineer who was "in the trenches", as she put it. Her record collection acted as a kind of job reference for a young woman who had experience working as a maintenance technician and assistant engineer.

"Sometimes on vinyl albums there would be a picture of the studio," she told Tape Op, "and I fantasized about being in that place where records were made. I didn't see myself in terms of what I would do there, because I didn't know, but it wasn't performing. Then I learned that there are people who make records …"

In a 2018 chat, Rogers told me: "When I joined Prince in 1983, it was my dream job. He had already put the wheels in motion to make the *Purple Rain* album and film, so I was fortunate enough to join him at that point. There was already quite a bit of momentum."

Thus she moved to Minneapolis to become Prince's technical accomplice – in the studio, on his movies and on the road. She was there nearly every day in his first commercial heyday when, for four glorious years until late 1987, everything he touched turned to purple.

"I was a fan of his music," said Rogers. "We lived on the same musical street, so to speak. If he would talk about Cameo or Rick James, Chic, the Gap Band, Sylvester, any of those R&B/disco artists, I knew the whole canon because that was the music that I enjoyed

too. So it helped that I was a Prince fan, I knew his musical references, I was an audio technician and I was a woman. All of that rolled into one package made me, in hindsight, ideally suited to work with him."

It's more than mere hindsight when Rogers looks back and acknowledges the sizzling cauldron of expressiveness that, in his mid-twenties, Prince now had on the boil. "He had to have recognized that he was a young man at his creative peak," she says. "He had to have been feeling not just the urgency of youth but the hubris and the mental swiftness, just like an athlete. I think an artistic athlete knows when he's at his peak as well.

"When Prince performed onstage, in the studio or in the privacy of his own home," she went on, "he always had the gas pedal floored. He

Opposite: Prince performs at the Ritz club in New York's East Village, in another image from 1981's Dirty Mind Tour.

Below: Returning home to Minneapolis, Prince plays a benefit concert for the Minnesota Dance Theater in 1983. This concert featured the first-ever live performance of 'Purple Rain'.

"A lot of people don't realize how much he gave for people." Morris Hayes

always worked at this high-performance output level." Soon, Rogers was able to make her own indispensable contribution, as the *Purple Rain* album began to take shape and form.

"The first song where I had a real comprehensive involvement was 'Let's Go Crazy', and that was in the fall of 1983," she said. "Things like 'Computer Blue' he worked out quite a bit. He recorded it in Minneapolis, in a studio that was in a warehouse there, but he also worked on that at Sunset Sound in Los Angeles.

"I was there in and out for parts of those things, I was there working on the movie. But as his full-time employee, he also had me working at home in Minneapolis with Jesse Johnson and members of The Time."

By the time Prince made his album debut in 1978, a young woman from Detroit named Marcella Levy was leaving her own fingerprints on the music scene. She had toured with Bob Seger, Leon Russell and Eric Clapton, singing with Slowhand himself on calling cards such as 'Promises', 'Wonderful Tonight' and 'Lay Down Sally'; and co-writing the latter. We would later know her as Marcella Detroit, one half of early 1990s chart-toppers Shakespears Sister.

"From the first minute I heard Prince's voice and his guitar playing, I was a fan, that was it," she said, in the documentary *Happy Birthday Prince*. "Moving forward to 1992, when I was in Shakespears Sister, we opened for him at this concert up in Glasgow, at an outdoor arena.

After the show, my manager said, 'Right before you did 'Stay', Prince brought the whole band to the wings and made everybody listen.' Had I known that, I would have been shaking in my boots.

"I became friends with his drummer, Michael Bland. We wrote a song together, he came to my studio, and he invited me to a few events he did with Prince. He was trying to arrange it so that Prince and I would meet, but unfortunately that never happened. I would have loved the opportunity to work with him. I feel the world is an emptier place without him. I miss his presence."

New Power Generation keyboard player Morris Hayes told Music Feeds: "A lot of people don't realize how much he gave for people. They knew about the money, they knew about the girls, they knew about the music, all that stuff. One side they didn't see, though, was how giving he was. He had his reasons, of course – he wanted to go about that side of things pretty quietly. He was so gracious about it, though. He was so supportive of his family, and all his band members.

"If we ever toured some place where one of us had grown up, he'd donate $100,000 to the school they went to. He'd never go public about it, never wanted to make a big deal about it. He cared so much about people – and for the longest time, it was off the record."

Back in the UK, the purple paladin was leaving his mark, or his symbol, on all who discovered him, in Wolverhampton, Edinburgh

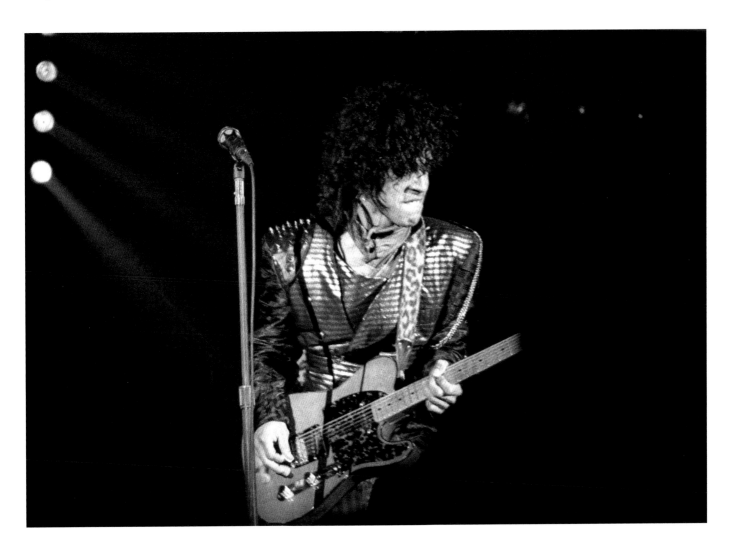

Above: British soul artist Beverley Knight, MBE, calls Prince the single biggest influence on her distinguished career.

and beyond. In the Midlands, the pre-teen Beverley Anne Smith was setting about her life's work of becoming a soul music fanatic. It would serve her well when she started to pursue her own performance muse, changed her name to Beverley Knight and developed a long career as one of Britain's greatest homegrown R&B talents. Not to mention the myriad charitable endeavours that helped toward her MBE in 2006.

As a young record buyer, Knight was first on her block to love Prince, and to notice lyrics that were as salacious as his music was trailblazing. "The first time I heard about this amazing person," she said, "was when I was round my grandma and grandad's house, which I would do every weekend without fail. My uncle Hayden couldn't sing a lick, but he was a huge fan of music and, luckily for me, good music. So he's the person I credit with broadening my musical tastes. I was very young – eight or nine.

"He had the room in the attic at grandma and grandad's," Beverley continued, "and he had tons of vinyl, he had a book on Dylan, he was just a man who loved music. Ahead of the curve, he'd managed to get MTV set up and he would play all these videos, and I'd sit and watch. The first thing I saw was this guy in a performance video wearing a purple mac with his band behind him, and he just mesmerized me. The song was 'Little Red Corvette' and I was thinking, 'Who *is* this? He's beautiful. The notes are beautiful, the sound is incredible', and I was absolutely hooked.

"My uncle had loads of vinyl by Prince, so it enabled me to go back to the *Dirty Mind* album, the *Prince* album, bits from *For You,* the very first album … so, ahead of most people, I was really getting into Prince. I had bragging rights. But he was risqué. From about the age of nine, there were things I did not understand that I loved, that went straight over my head. By the time I got to 14, 15, when Prince was doing *Sign o' The Times* and *Lovesexy,* I was like, 'Oh, that's what he meant.'

"Then revisiting some of the earlier records … songs like 'Head': you're a ten-year-old, you haven't got a clue. Then they all make sense when you're a teenager and you go, 'I can't believe he said that!' But he was clever. He was near the knuckle, but he was clever.

"If he wasn't speaking about things in an allegorical way, on occasion he would drop the odd word that would make you sit up straight. But otherwise he would allude to sex and all things sexual in way that almost had a spirituality behind it, if you could put two things like that together. I guess Marvin Gaye did that as well, before Prince.

"He managed to talk about sex but he would package it in a perfect pop way. 'Little Red Corvette' is a perfect pop record, but he's talking about condoms and stuff. He was so majestic in the way he would talk about things.

"After that, when I heard the rest of *1999,* I thought it was extraordinary, and when *Purple Rain* dropped, that was it. The whole world became

Prince-crazy and my interest in him spilled into total fangirling obsession. I followed him everywhere a young girl was able to."

Knight's account of a pre-pubescent attraction to Prince that she herself didn't fully understand has a remarkable echo in the memories of another future star and similarly magnetic performer, Scottish singer-songwriter KT Tunstall. "I remember being 14 years old, and my dad finally capitulated to getting a satellite dish in the house," she said in *Happy Birthday Prince*. "Then ensued our battle between the sports channel and MTV.

"I'm sure I'd heard Prince on the radio and it had permeated to television. But the first time I really remember engaging with his music was seeing the video for 'Raspberry Beret', which remains my favourite song of his because of that, I think.

"I was completely glued. I'd never seen anyone who looked like that. The music was so melodic and simple, it was this brilliant melody that you could sing back immediately, but this amazing funk and soul to the track. It was very sexy, it was a very sensual video – even though I don't think there's any bare flesh in the video, really – but he's such a sensual performer. I think the first time you saw Prince, you knew that

he was one of the greatest musicians."

Tunstall came to realize that her early idol was decades ahead of his time, not only in the way he made his music but in the way he lived. As the late 2010s brought us to a time of supposed enlightenment about sexual identity, she could only smile. "I was an 80s kid, which I will be forever grateful for," she said. "It was such a brilliant decade to come of age.

"It's really strange sitting here watching everyone make such a fuss about gender fluidity and cross-dressing. We're in a place where real steps are being taken for equality, and that's an excellent and necessary thing. But it's almost like people are more outraged now than they were in the 80s. Me growing up, I remember *all* the guys were dressing like girls, and all the girls were dressing like guys. Madonna was doing stuff that Miley Cyrus would *never* do, and Sinéad O'Connor was burning pictures of the Pope.

Below, left: BRIT and Ivor Novello Award-winning Scottish singer-songwriter KT Tunstall, who recalls hearing 'Raspberry Beret' for the first time as a teenager.

Below, right: Shakespears Sister, who made waves with their alternative pop-rock mix in the late 80s and early 90s, also fell under Prince's spell.

"It was a time where there was a lot of courage in pop music," she went on. "There was a lot of freedom in the way that people expressed themselves, and Prince was such a beautiful, genius example of all of that. No one was going 'Is he gay? Is he straight? Is he this, is he that?' They were going 'He's Prince. He does what he wants.' You don't need to ask the question, just watch and be amazed.

"I don't know if I was really aware of Little Richard growing up. He was probably something I came to later, and I was so delighted seeing where some of Prince's inspiration had come from.

"As a musician myself," Tunstall concluded, "or even if you're not a musician, just watching someone completely unshackled by self-doubt in any way, and having an idea and actioning it without limit, is an amazing and powerful thing to witness. David Bowie did that. Michael Jackson was another one. But Prince's appeal is so deep. His music demands that you follow him. It's not a background soundtrack to your life, it's going to take you somewhere that you weren't expecting to go."

Above: Prince accepts an Oscar for Best Original Song Score for 'Purple Rain', flanked by Revolution band members Wendy Melvoin and Lisa Coleman.

Opposite: Prince performs at the Auditorium Theater in Chicago in 1983, as the *1999* album propels him further into the public consciousness.

"The music, for me, doesn't come on a schedule. I don't know when it's going to come, and when it does, I want it out." Prince

Left: A platinum disc for one million US sales of *Controversy*.
Above: Tambourines bearing Prince logos.
Below: Reel-to-reel tapes circa 1982–86 containing such hits as '1999,' 'Let's Go Crazy' and 'Kiss'.
Opposite: Two typically understated stage outfits.

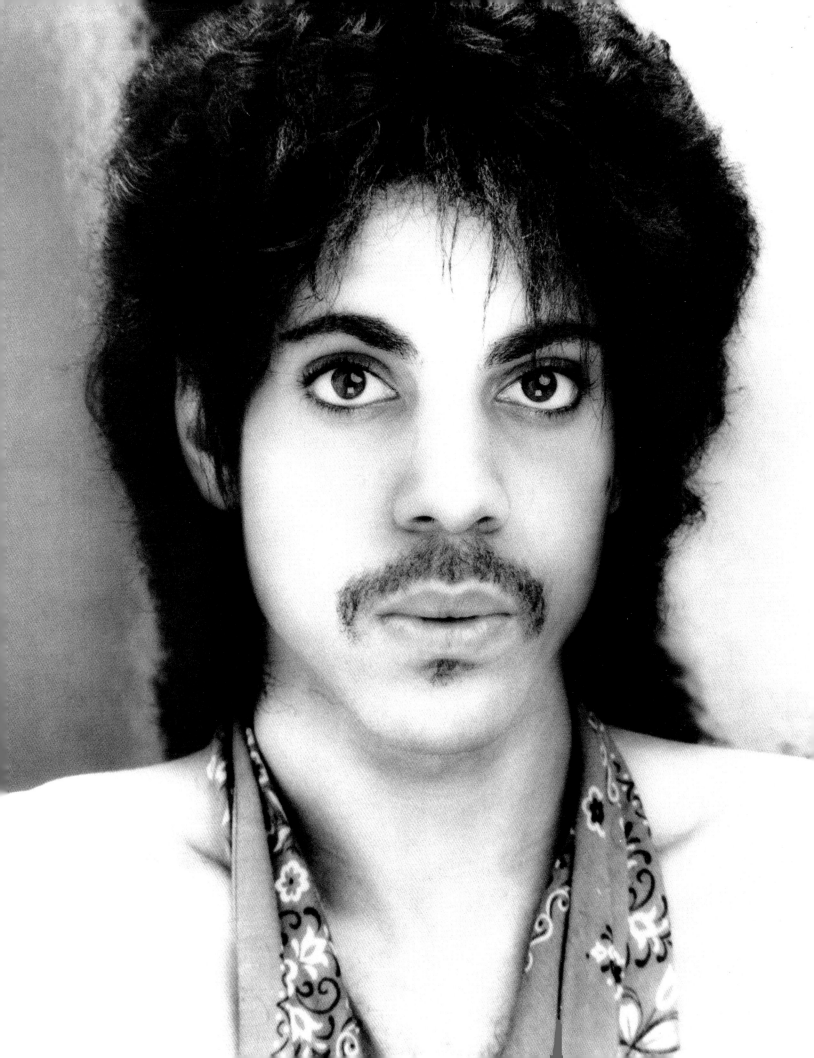

CHAPTER THREE

BECOMING PRINCE

Opposite: Prince photographed up
close and personal in 1981.

Prince was so far beyond his years in talent, it's easy to forget that he was still a teenager who enjoyed playing pranks, even as he began to attract record company interest. During an interview with the *Minnesota Daily*, published in April 1977, he orders a milkshake, adds ketchup, steak sauce, jam and other condiments, gives it to the waitress and says, "I think there's something wrong with this. It tastes funny."

Above: Prince turns up the temperature in 1981, wearing little more than a guitar.

Right: Prince cuts a cool pose backstage at the Paradiso, Amsterdam, the Netherlands.

By the time his rise to royalty was inarguable, Susannah Melvoin was well placed to witness his creative and personal blossoming. Plenty precocious herself, by her late teens she was working in Los Angeles as a session singer, and for David Geffen and MCA Music Publishing. From an initial role as musically connected fangirl, admiring him from not so far away, she soon found herself living with him.

"What drew us all together," she told me, "was our deep love of music, and we all played. We came to his party with a different musical palette, and it obviously moved him in ways that sparked another kind of musical expression for him. Wendy and Lisa had chord structures that were deep and layered, and brought something to him in that way. Soon after Wendy and Lisa were there, I came into it as a singer.

"At the time, I was working with Quincy Jones, and Prince had heard something I did, at our house. Wendy, Lisa and I lived together and he would come and stay at our place. We'd go pick him up at the airport, bring him back to the house and we started there, as not only musical brothers and sisters, maybe, but we also became really close as family.

"He got to be in a family of three women, and we got to have our Prince. It was really amazing, because not that many people had that kind of relationship with him. The shyness came from his lack of interest in socializing."

"I'm really free and open once I get to know a person," Prince told the *Minneapolis Star Tribune* in early 1979. "But when I first encounter something, I'm a little laid back and cautious. People constantly call me shy. I don't feel shy, but I guess I sometimes come off that way to people."

But even when he played his much-heralded hometown debut on January 5 of that year, in the first of two nights at the Capri Theater, the disconnect between private caution and public abandon was evident. Dressed like Jimi Hendrix, and in his first public performance since high school, he and his band delivered a rock-funk riot of a show. His pre-Revolution band featured Cymone and other early believers Bobby Z., Matt Fink, Gayle Chapman and Dez Dickerson.

"Prince's first concert is energetic, sexy", ran the headline of the lead review in the Entertainment section of the *Star Tribune* on January 8. "He had the opportunity to play his first concert in New York's prestigious, 20,000-seater Madison Square Garden," wrote Jon Bream. "But instead Prince, the teen-aged, one-man-band recording star, chose to debut at the Capri Theater, an obscure movie house in his home town of Minneapolis."

Still only 20, with the debut album out and another 20 songs in his pocket for the impending, self-titled follow-up, Prince was already moving those around him to hyperbole. Local DJ Kyle Ray fronted

the Capri show with frenetic chutzpah straight out of the James Brown playbook when he introduced the new sensation: "The power and the glory, the Minneapolis story … Prince!"

"A little rough around the edges, but certainly the beginning of something that we could learn from," said Bobby Z. of the shows. "And Prince became better and better and better, until he polished the edges off into a shining diamond."

Gayle Chapman, who played keyboards in the band before Lisa Coleman's arrival, remains an unsung element of Prince's first flowering of fame. Born in San Diego, she grew up in Minnesota and met her erstwhile bandleader through a combination of local contacts and cosmic intervention. In 2019, she told Scott Goldfine on funknstuff.net's Truth in Rhythm video series that she was listening with rapt attention to Prince's debut album *For You* when she had a supernatural experience.

"A voice spoke to me," she said, "that came down [from] the sky, through my head and out the other side and it said, 'In order for him to tour, he's going to need a band.' I turned the music down and looked around and went, 'I heard that!'" Investigations revealed that Prince was indeed auditioning for his first live group. His cousin, Charles Smith, was a friend of Gayle's and got her in. Her next move was nothing if not challenging for her, and revealing for us to eavesdrop on.

Opposite: Prince makes like one of his forebears, Jimi Hendrix, at the Paradiso show in 1981.

Below: Prince was his own revolution, leading the gender-bending style that characterized the pop scene of the 1980s.

"I remember going to his house … and he was nowhere to be seen because he was downstairs with André and Bobby, doing auditions," said Chapman. "All of these people were in the room, and most of them were young ladies. They were all dressed to the nines. I was wearing a blue jean dress, flip-flops and a headscarf! I'm going 'Oh sh**, I'm kind of out of luck here!'"

But she headed to the keyboard, held her nerve, followed their groove, led them into a jam of her own and went home. She heard nothing for three months. "I was taking a nap one afternoon and I got a phone call and it was Prince. He said in that lovely monotone voice of his, 'HelloGaylethisisPrincewhatareyoudoingrightnow?' 'Well, I was sleeping, but how are you?' He invited me to rehearsal, I showed up an hour later and that's how that started."

Even then, the image of the utterly driven frontman was so much at odds with the retiring homeboy. "The music end of my life I'll probably always do, but not the business end," he told Martin Keller in the *Twin Cities Reader*, immediately after that Capri Theater debut. "I hate plane rides. I'd rather stay at home and rehearse, or play in the studio by myself.

"I like the quiet here in Minneapolis, and nobody bothers me; I'll always keep a place here," he went on. "I'd rather hear loud, live music if I go out at all. Actually, I spend a lot of time in the bathtub thinking. Music and playing is almost like breathing for me."

By the release in 1981 of his fourth album *Controversy*, Prince may have been growing ever more remote from the machinery of the music business, but his lyrics exhibited no such coyness. *Rolling Stone* observed that where his first three records were "erotically self-absorbed", now he was proclaiming "unfettered sexuality".

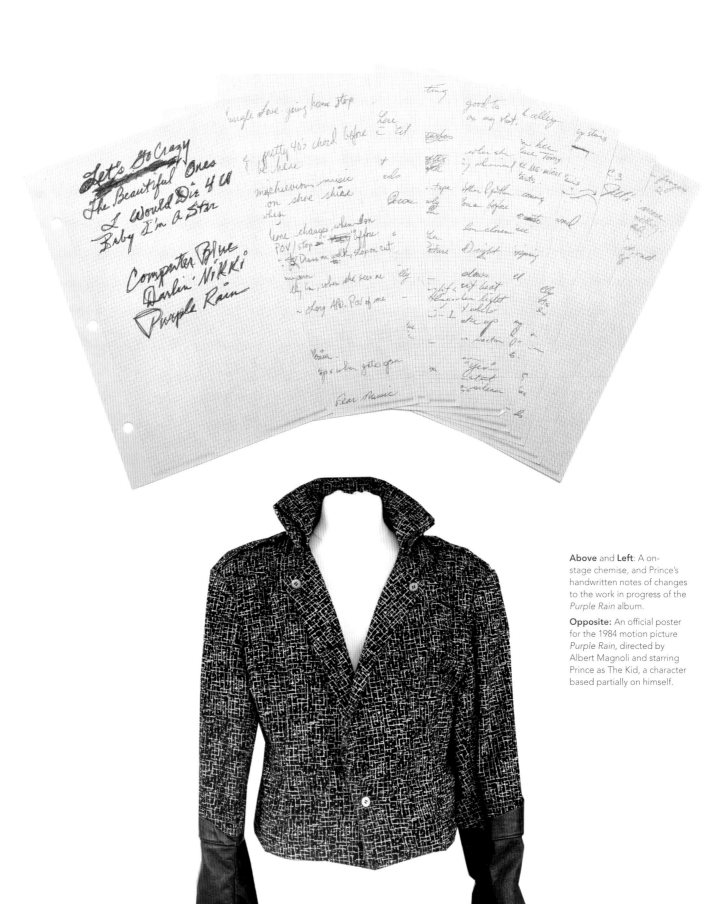

Above and **Left**: A on-stage chemise, and Prince's handwritten notes of changes to the work in progress of the *Purple Rain* album.

Opposite: An official poster for the 1984 motion picture *Purple Rain*, directed by Albert Magnoli and starring Prince as The Kid, a character based partially on himself.

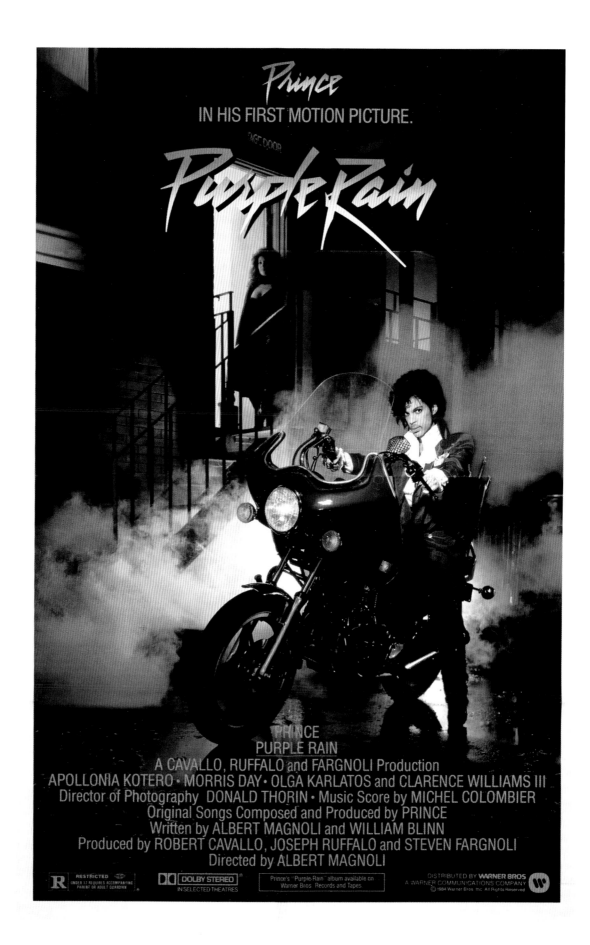

So what was it like working, often as the only other person in the studio, on those early, sexed-up songs? Before, and segueing into, the days of Prince's close working bond with Susan Rogers, the woman in that role from 1981 to 1986 was Peggy McCreary. She had become used to working among the famous when she waited tables at the Roxy on Sunset Strip, before taking an engineering class and getting the gopher job at Sunset Sound studio. She watched, and learned, and soon a certain 23-year-old arrived in her life.

"Hollywood Sound had technical difficulties and their board went down," McCreary remembered in a 2019 interview with *Pitchfork*. "They called Sunset and said, 'Do you have an engineer and a room available this weekend?' And I was available with a room, but the receptionist said, 'Peggy can't work alone in the studio on the weekend with him. He writes really dirty songs about giving head and stuff.'

"I thought, 'Oh god, who's gonna be walking into the studio?' So I was prepared for something different than the person that walked in, who was small and polite and extremely quiet. He would mumble what he needed from behind a flap of hair.

"I said, 'You know what? If you want me to work with you, you're going to have to talk to me, to my face, so I can hear you!' That was on *Controversy*, and we finished that album, and I thought, 'I'll never work with this guy again.' But when he came back for *1999*, he requested me."

His lack of demonstrative appreciation of others could be almost studied. "I remember after *1999*," said McCreary, "which was just me and him in the studio (we were working on Vanity 6, I think). I said, 'Do you like my work?' And he looked at me like, 'You're here, aren't you?' That's all you ever got from him."

New Power Generation keyboard player Tommy Barbarella identified with Prince's outsider image long before they worked together. "He made it OK to be different, and not only that, he made it cool to be different," he told me. "He connected with a lot of people on the fringe, people who didn't quite fit in. He made it OK. It was like, 'If no one else gets me, Prince gets me.'"

This was a person who affected and impressed artists from way beyond his wheelhouse, and always will. One time, in an energizing and epic conversation in Santa Monica, the distinguished singer-songwriter Jackson Browne and I fell into spontaneous dialogue that went on for so long, he missed his next appointment.

At one point, comparing his own *modus operandi* to those of others, he mused: "You want the things you sing about to be about life and other people's lives. If I shut myself away and tried to ramp up the output, it might limit the interest I take in things that are pretty universal. On the other hand, some of the best music ever made has been made that way, whether it's Prince or Keith Richards. People who are completely wrapped up in the music."

That was the Prince that Susannah Melvoin knew, but she got closer than most. "He specifically wanted to appear like the man in the woods, the hermit, just not speaking to anybody," she said. "He had no desire, there was no need to. Wendy and Lisa and myself were very close to him. Once he did know you," she laughed, "he had no problem whatsoever expressing himself, in any way."

Above: New Generation keyboardist Tommy Barbarella identified with Prince's unique image.

Opposite: Susannah Melvoin in front of a Prince portrait in 2019. As a member of the Paisley Park-signed band The Family and later The Revolution of the line-up, she worked closely with Prince during his wave of creative genius of the mid-to-late 1980s.

CHAPTER FOUR

PRINCE AND THE PENGUIN

Opposite: Prince performs on the Purple Rain Tour at Joe Louis Arena in Detroit, Michigan, on November 8, 1984. The purple jacket and white frilly shirt are still visual shorthand for a peerless performer.

Prince's sound engineer of the classic 1980s period, Susan Rogers — "engineer" sounds inadequate to describe her supremely astute contribution to his work, as running mate and sounding board — painted me a hilarious picture of life on the road in those days. It was a perfect thumbnail of the madness of touring in that rarefied atmosphere and, above all, it showed how funny Prince could be. The year was 1985, the tour the lead-up to his seventh studio album.

"He had a great sense of joy and optimism, and he had a great laugh," Rogers said. "When he laughed, it was deep, a chest laugh. It was real, he never had a fake laugh. He had alternative characters, voices that he would adopt. One of them must have been patterned after his father. It was an elderly, black, wizened sage.

"He also had kind of a smartass character voice, very similar to Morris Day and how he was portrayed in the *Purple Rain* movie. So Prince could be very biting and nasty in his humor, sometimes it was the equivalent of a 13- or 14-year-old boy. But maybe that's not so uncommon for men," she laughed.

"It could be schoolyard humor sometimes, which wasn't all that funny if you were on the receiving end of it. But in general, Prince really loved to laugh and was generally a very happy person. I imagine that he would have regarded depression as being self-pitying."

So to the in-joke that he came to share with Rogers. "It became a bit of a challenge to see who could stay awake the longest, but I was *determined* I was not going to lose that challenge," she said. "I was very privileged to be working for him. I was just about two years older than he, but I could match him, I could stay up as long as he did, through sheer determination and willpower. Nothing stops pure pure persistence, and we both had it in those days."

At this point, an improbable stuffed toy enters the picture. "On the Purple Rain Tour," Rogers recalled, "there was a token that we had. It was a gift that someone had given Prince, a very large stuffed penguin, about three or four feet tall. It was a very sombre-looking animal, very formal, meticulously groomed. He had a little purple bow tie and black wings, but sprinkled with rhinestones.

"We had it on the tour with us and we really didn't know what to do with it. We carted it around; it lived in a road case. At some point on the tour, the road crew began using that penguin to capture people who were asleep on the job. Back in the 80s we had Polaroid cameras, and we needed them to document certain [mix] set-ups so that you could reproduce that set-up the next day.

"Sometimes a member of the road crew would be passed out asleep on a road case. Another member of the road crew would set the penguin right on him and then snap a Polaroid. So we began saving these Polaroids. One of the big road cases had a lid that would lift up, and on the inside of the lid were all the Polaroids of all the crew members who had been caught sleeping.

"It started to turn into a contest," Susan went on, "because we were working brutal hours, and it was a *long* tour. Eventually we had Polaroids of *everyone* in that road case, and there were only two people [left] standing, and it was Prince … and me. We were the only two that hadn't been caught by that damned penguin."

This chimes precisely with a comment made by Rogers' boss around that same time, in the days when he was still granting the occasional interview. "I swear to God it's not out of boldness when I say this," he confided, "but there's not a person around who can stay awake as long as I can. Music is what keeps me awake."

Rogers continued the story. "Everyone else had a photo of themselves passed out on the desk or on their instrument, on the cases, backstage or wherever with that penguin," she said. "But no one had caught us yet, and he and I were like, eye to eye. 'You're going down.' 'Not me, *you're* going down.'

"So it was the end of the tour, we were at Sunset Sound in Los

Angeles and we had just finished sequencing the *Around the World in a Day* album. The tour had ended but we'd been recording the album as the tour went along. Prince had his band there, and there were some invited guests, which was rare for the studio. Usually, as he would say, there would be 'No non-combatants'.

"But in this case there were visitors there, so there weren't enough chairs to go around. I'd been up for at least a day, and probably two days, with no sleep, so I was sitting in the control room at Sunset Sound with my back to the wall and we were listening back to the playback of this album.

"I was sitting there with my eyes closed and I heard, 'Click! Vrrrr' … It was the unmistakeable sound of that Polaroid camera. I opened my eyes and went, 'No! No! I wasn't sleeping, I wasn't sleeping!' and there was that stupid penguin right next to me, and Prince was standing there with the camera. I jumped up and I said, 'no! Not fair! I wasn't sleeping, my eyes were closed!' So officially I lost the contest, but unofficially I didn't.

"It's funny how tame our 'antics' sound compared with the typical rock 'n' roll debaucheries, but I'm proud of that," said Susan. "Prince had a sterling work ethic and wasn't the type to

destroy hotel rooms or get high and vandalize equipment. In those days, our fun was the good, clean variety. That fostered a greater atmosphere of trust and respect compared to those musical families where bacchanalia was the norm."

Then Rogers remembered the prequel to her punchline. "Just a matter of hours before he caught me, I nearly caught him," she chuckled. "We were not allowed to take photos of Prince. We had signed this agreement, and he was very private and controlling about that, so we were all good.

"But we were working on this record, he was in the chair at the console, and he was doing the same thing that I would ultimately be doing a few hours later. He was sitting there listening with his eyes closed. And I thought, 'I got him!' So I snuck up behind him and I pushed that penguin across the floor. I wanted to get it right behind him and right near his elbow.

"I had the camera and I was bringing it up and moving as slowly and quietly as I could, and bringing the camera up and the penguin's right there, and I'm lining up my shot … and then he says, '*Who do you think you're going to get with that?*' Ohhh, he had eyes in the back of his head. I nearly got him, but I didn't. He won. Of course he won."

Below: Prince checks himself backstage during the 1984 Purple Rain Tour. His road crew would take pictures of those that fell asleep on the itinerary, but not even his almost equally indefatigable engineer Susan Rogers could ever quite snap him with his eyes closed.

Clockwise from bottom: The headband worn by Prince in *Purple Rain*; set list and Itinerary from the tour of the same name; gloves, boots and outfit worn by Prince in the film.

CHAPTER FIVE

THE FAMILY THAT PLAYS TOGETHER

Opposite: In the moment. Prince live on stage circa 1985, conquering the world with The Revolution.

Of all the fabulously talented artists that passed through the doors of Paisley Park, one act had a particularly direct line to Prince. The story of The Family remained largely unknown by a wider congregation, but was written partly by some individuals with close creative and personal connections to him, both in the 1980s and in the latter part of his life.

In August 1985, the group's self-titled LP became the first release by an act signed to Paisley Park. Even by the high standards the boss demanded, it was a beacon of understated chic and supremely tasteful funk and soul. Written by – but not fully credited to – Prince, it featured vocals by The Family's double-bill vocal pairing of Susannah Melvoin (Wendy's sister) and Twin Cities soulboy St. Paul Peterson, who Prince discovered at the age of 17.

It was also the album featuring the original (and, to these ears, superior) version of Prince's tear-stained ballad 'Nothing Compares 2 U'. Melvoin remained ambivalent over whether the song was about her, as his intimate of the time, but told me that others were certain it was. *The Family* album did produce one substantial US R&B hit; but 'Nothing Compares 2 U' wasn't it. Never released as a single, that remained largely overlooked until Sinéad O'Connor got to it at the end of the decade.

The Minneapolis outfit scored instead with 'Screams Of Passion', but while the album was no sales disaster and made the R&B Top 20, it hardly demanded a follow-up. Paisley Park was not yet fully formed, existing for now only as an offshoot of Warner Bros. It had no staff of its own and certainly no futuristic headquarters. Yet.

By the time a sequel was mooted, Prince was away to France to star in his directorial debut movie *Under the Cherry Moon*. Peterson split the scene and the other members of the group became part of The Revolution. In one of the great might-have-beens of those years, it left behind the prospect of a Paisley Park Tour that was to have featured The Family along with fellow travellers Sheila E., Mazarati and Taja Sevelle. That would have been something to witness.

Twenty-six years on, in September 2011, I flew to Minneapolis to meet The Family as they reunited for a thoroughly superior hometown gig at the Loring Theater, marking the release of their hugely belated second coming. The excellent *Gaslight* album appeared, for what we will call legal reasons, under the new group name fDeluxe.

But there was no concealing that the interim quarter-century had

Left: Prince and The Revolution perform with Ronnie Wood at Prince's first-ever European aftershow. The jam took place at Busby's in London after a Wembley concert in August 1986 and also featured Nile Rodgers, (not pictured here).

only turned ingénue prospects into seasoned stylists. Their particular relevance to our story is in their maturation from instruments of their "creator" (Peterson's word) into a fully formed band in their own right.

"He was the author, we were the characters in that book," said Susannah Melvoin, on the eve of *Gaslight*'s release. "They just weren't realized. This book didn't get read; it just sat as a transcript. Now it's out there with the hard cover and it's got an ending. So we can get out there now and fully realize what this could have been."

Peterson later added: "We had lived our own lives and had our own successes and failures and a story to tell. In our own words, instead of his words."

Eric Leeds, who had a decade more experience than his bandmates, offered me his observations on the frontman he knew. "You have to remember that Prince looks at all of his music, in his whole life, as a movie, and everybody who's involved with him on whatever level is a character in his movie.

"When he started to hit it big, he was very concerned from a business standpoint, being a black artist who was also much more eclectic than what we just think of as an R&B artist – because of the rock influences, the folk influences – and he had very good reason not to want to be pigeonholed as 'the biggest black artist'. He wanted to be the biggest *pop* artist. His R&B side was a major part of who he is, but he did not want to be identified only with that.

"That's why he created The Time. That was going to be the creative outlet for that. The Morris Day character? That's Prince. I've sat in a room and seen Prince be Morris Day better than Morris Day."

The first iteration of The Time had substantial US success with three albums produced, supposedly incognito, by Prince, and a quartet of Top 10 soul hits from them including 'Get It Up' and '777-9311'. Jellybean Johnson was an original member. Later, Peterson and Jerome Benton joined too, before all three were cast in The Family, whose very existence, according to Leeds, was born of The Time's disintegration. Prince would now flesh out the R&B leanings of the first group in the second.

"When [The Time] fell apart, he still wanted to have a creative outlet that was going to be kind of like that. It was, 'How can I take that and make it work?' and he came up with this concept of making it street-oriented, R&B/funk influenced, but a little more pop-ish. Because it was the first time he was going to use a real horn [Leeds's saxophones], he looked at more of a jazzy flavor.

"You look back at the first album," Leeds went on. "The idea [was]

Opposite: An airborne Prince performs on stage on the Parade Tour, Wembley Arena, London, August 1986.

Above: Prince during the 1986 Parade Tour with singer-percussionist Sheila E, a familiar part of the Paisley Park circle of the period, whose solo hits included the Prince composition 'The Glamorous Life'.

Above: The only known cassette copy of the *Black Album*, which was withdrawn from release in 1987 and finally appeared in 1994.

Below: The CD cover of the *Emancipation* album, released in 1996 as Prince embarked on a new business model.

we're going to be this crazy bunch of interracial, almost nouveau-riche [people], hanging out in a big mansion in our pyjamas. But we're still going to be funky. It was as much a Prince album as anything else he was about. Everybody knows that the music was his, so we were playing roles."

By the release of the similarly undervalued *Gaslight*, the musicians had come of age. "Now we've graduated," said Leeds. "We're the producers, directors and screenwriters." "It's almost like we're finishing what we started," added Peterson. "It's like fruition."

In 2014, fDeluxe rose again with the covers album *AM Static,* which was confident and eclectic enough to swing from Eric Carmen's 'All By Myself' to the Rolling Stones's 'Miss You'. Since then, Peterson has maintained the highest profile, as an in-demand session player, performing with his and Leeds's LP Music project (Leeds/Peterson), and on three 2019 singles of his own, including a suitably funky celebration of his home town, 'Minne Forget Me Not'.

Talking again immediately after Prince's death, Peterson told me how vehemently the superstar had opposed the idea of his former charges using their original band name. "We had a personal conversation about it," said Peterson, "and he was adamant that we wouldn't use the name, since the main person [Prince] wasn't involved in anything new we were conceiving. He was concerned that the legacy of the group 'not be tarnished'.

"I, of course, didn't see it that way. We were of the opinion that we were 'continuing the legacy'. He still wanted control of the situation, and we decided it was simply in our best interest to change the name; thus fDeluxe was born."

It's delightful to report that the story had a happy ending and two poignant reunions. In March 2016, just a few weeks before his death, Prince came to see Leeds and Peterson in their new project, LP Music, at a Minneapolis club.

Six months before that meeting, Prince had invited Peterson and Leeds to play at Paisley Park for the launch of his *Hit n Run Phase One* album. When they arrived, he embraced them with all the warmth you would hope. "It was nice to give him a squeeze," Peterson said on social media, "tell him thank you, and be back at Paisley one last time."

Below: Prince soars during what is essentially a public rehearsal (tickets: $5) for his Parade Tour, at the hometown venue First Avenue, Minneapolis, in 1986.

COACHELL

CHAPTER SIX
SIGN O' THE GENIUS

Opposite: An eye-catching poster, commissioned from South American artist Pablo Lobato, for Prince's headlining appearance at the 2008 Coachella Festival. The epic show included covers of Radiohead's 'Creep' and songs by Santana and The Beatles.

Few people had the opportunity to watch Prince's creativity spark in quite the way that Susannah Melvoin did. During their times together in the 1980s, she was able to watch one particular song grow from seed to signature. And not just any song or any subject. A hugely gifted singer and songwriter herself, she went on to be an important component of the ensuing album in her own right.

"**Y**ou know the one [song] that sums up his brilliance, when I hear it on the radio?" she said to me in 2017. "'Sign o' the Times'. I remember it perfectly when it was recorded, and being with him at the time. He and I were in LA and we were at our hotel, and there was an earthquake. He'd never really experienced it before." Melvoin was a native of California, so had the advantage of him, "although I don't like them at all, they scare the pants off me.

"The hotel started to shake and sway. He was like, 'We're out, we have *got* to go back to Minneapolis.' That following morning, we got a newspaper and it was, 'In France a skinny man died of a big disease.' It was on the cover of the *LA Times*. The AIDS epidemic was completely out. It wasn't a hidden conversation. Everybody needed to do something about it." One remembers that in the all-too-realistic second half of Prince's resulting couplet, the man's girlfriend finds his needle, and falls victim to the same terrible infection.

"So he was *lit*," said Melvoin, "with such intense feelings about his environment, the world at large, mortality, being the man that he would become. We went back to Minneapolis and he wrote that. That was the moment for real that I witnessed what he did and what he could do, when he got incredibly moved by something, then he would create from it.

"Whenever I hear it I think, 'I know where that was done.' I know where his head was at, his heart, his ears. *That* is how that song is created.

That is the man that I know, the creative person that I do know and that everyone should know. He was a layered, complicated creature."

Another close associate from Prince's early days who was afforded an early listen to the staging-post *Sign o' the Times* double album was his early bandmate André Cymone. "I never looked at him as the immense superstar that he became until, like … now," he told me poignantly in 2017, after his old friend's death. "But there were a couple of times [when] he'd reach out and say, 'Man, you want to come to this gig?'

"He invited me to the house and he played me *Sign o' the Times*. He would do that from time to time when he had a record, and he would want me to hear what he was doing. It was kind of how we used to do [it] when he lived at my mom's house. He played me this album and it was unbelievable. I remember my favorite songs were 'The Ballad Of Dorothy Parker' and 'Sign o' the Times'. It just seemed like it was never-ending.

Above: Prince poses with his band during his Lovesexy Tour at Feyenoord Stadium in August 1988 in Rotterdam, the Netherlands. Group members included Sheila E, Eric Leeds and Cat.

Opposite: A poster for the *Sign o' The Times* concert movie. Susannah Melvoin vividly remembers the creation of the title song, written while they were in Los Angeles during an earthquake.

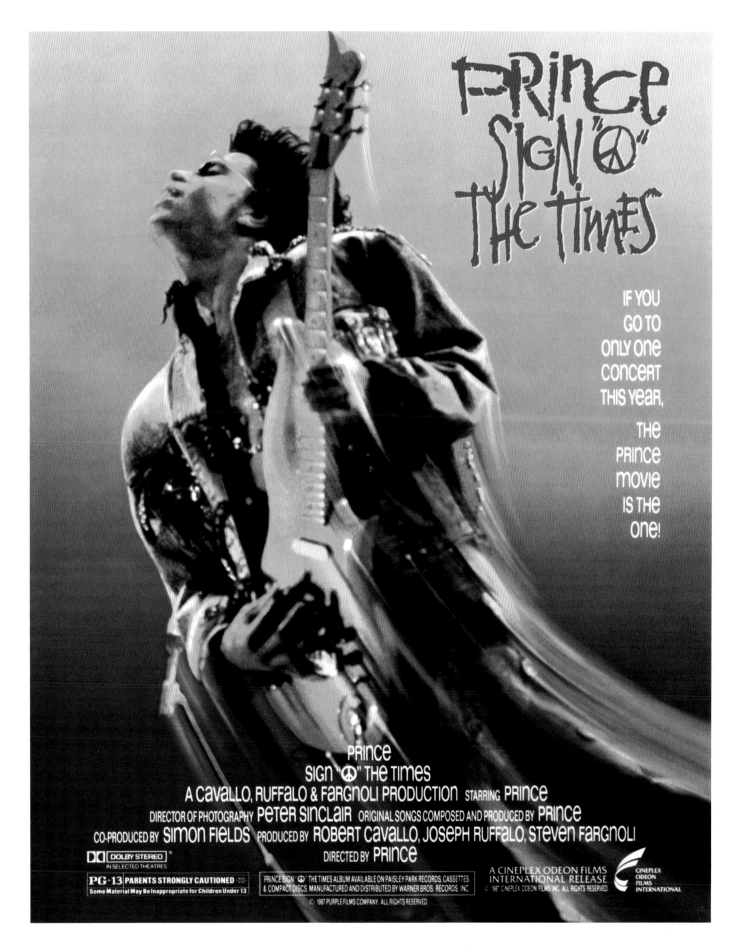

Left: Prince performs at Bunker's Music Bar & Grill in Minneapolis, Minnesota, on April 4, 1988. He would often call into the venue for a live jam.

Opposite, above: Prince's personally-owned set centre cap inserts from his Bentley.

Opposite, below: A poster for June 1987's four-night stand at Palatrussardi, the arena in Milan, during the Sign o' The Times Tour.

"I remember there was one of those big, oversized clocks on the wall, and I had no choice but to sit there and watch the hours go by," laughed Cymone. "But after it was all done, he was like, 'What do you think?' He had just put out something not that long ago, and I said, 'You might not want to give people all of that, because that's a lot of cool stuff, you might want to break it up, and he said, 'Man, I can't do that. When I record this stuff, I've got to get it out.' He was very adamant about that."

The 'Sign o' the Times' single was released in February 1987, six weeks ahead of the album of the same name, which became the most lauded record Prince ever made. Sixteen songs strong, it was hailed as a masterpiece, his *What's Going On?*; even a cultural revolution of its own. It was at once retro-psychedelic and quasi-futuristic. Many called it the best album of the 1980s. On his death, the Minneapolis *Star Tribune* called it "the most perfect balance of everything Prince: grinding funk, catchy pop, anthemic rock, tender balladry."

Another of the album's highlights, 'Starfish and Coffee', did more than just feature Melvoin on backing vocals. "We wrote that together," she said. "It's a really important song [because] it represents an important part of him that runs deep. His love of the kooky kid in everybody, and the stories of Cynthia Rose, who I went to school with."

"It's this young girl who was on the spectrum, although no one knew what that was at the time," Melvoin explained. "We were in school. But she's our hero in this. He would ask me quite often to tell the story of how Wendy and I grew up with her. We had six years of being in a classroom with this girl, from first grade to sixth grade. It's a true story, it's real." In the lyric, Cynthia is a model of freethinking, right down to the playful detail of her breakfasts.

Melvoin writes with equal candour and radiance on her starfishandcoffeeofficial.com, a trove for Prince devotees with its unimpeachable first-hand detail of the period. "I remember fall in Minneapolis vividly," she muses on that platform. "The air smells like water and earth and the lakes that spread throughout the city become deserted of people, they now walk around the lakes bundled up in what is the last fall jacket one can get away with wearing. I loved it and I loved what was to be an extremely beautiful time in my life."

She describes the day that she and Prince wrote the song. "Sitting around the kitchen table was Prince, his engineer Susan Rogers and myself. It was a time Susan and I spent every day with him either recording or keeping each other company. Prince and I spent many hours together, either in the studio working, or driving around Minneapolis talking to each other and listening to music.

"It was this fall afternoon in Minnesota at our kitchen table when Prince came up the stairs from his studio, sat next to me and asked if I would to tell him the whole story of Cynthia Rose in detail. A few hours later he asked if I'd write it down.

"On that afternoon when Prince asked if I'd write this story, I would have no idea what was about to transpire downstairs in his studio. Prince requested that I not go downstairs until he was finished with the track. Ten hours later, Susan came upstairs to get me. I walked into the studio, Prince was standing at the console with a tired, gentle smile on his face and said, 'Here it is!'"

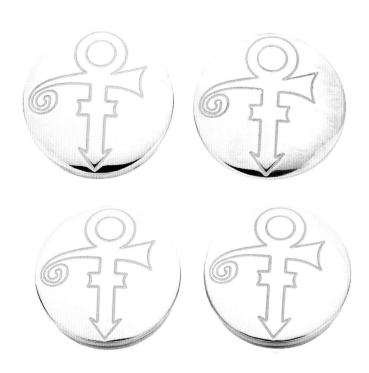

CHAPTER SEVEN

MY NAME IS PRINCE,

HIS NAME WAS LUKA

Opposite: A studio portrait of Suzanne Vega. Prince personally wrote to the Californian artist to say that her song 'Luka' was "the most compelling piece of music I've heard in a long time".

She didn't make anything of it for years, but the distinguished singer-songwriter Suzanne Vega owns a very personal piece of Prince ephemera. The Californian composer and performer only decided to tell her fans about it when she heard of the death of her contemporary inspiration. When she did, on April 25, 2016, her own audience and the wider world were taken with an act of private appreciation from one artist to another.

"I have a strange and compelling connection with Prince, in that he wrote me a handwritten letter back in 1987, because he loved the song 'Luka'," she said, in an interview featured in my *Prince and Me* documentary for BBC Radio 2. "I must have got it through my manager. I think he said, 'This one's really special,' and he sent it down to my house.

"It's in ink, on beautiful paper with a flower, and it says, 'Dearest Suzanne, 'Luka' is the most compelling piece of music I've heard in a long time. I thank God 4 u.' And he signs it Prince. His handwriting is as beautiful and florid as you would imagine, and there's a little flower that he draws on it."

'Luka', from Vega's second album *Solitude Standing*, was released as a single in April 1987, and told a chilling tale of domestic abuse that was in stark contrast to the gentle beauty of its melody. Prince's note arrived on headed paper giving Prince's address in Chanhassen, Minnesota, and his telephone number. "There are no words 2 tell you all the things I feel when I hear it," he added.

"I was so moved by this," said Vega, "and so taken with the beauty of the paper, that I framed it and had it on my wall for years, until it started to fade. So when he died, I took a picture of it and put it up for my fans to see." The post stated matter-of-factly: "I found my letter from #Prince." To her surprise, 70,000 people gave it the thumbs up.

At the ASCAP Awards, soon after Prince's passing, Vega told *Us Weekly* and other reporters that, after having the letter in a frame for years, she noticed that its original colour was draining. "So I took it down and put it in my scrapbook," she explained. "It was on my wall for so long, and a part of my life for so long, that I don't remember that actual moment when I received it. But it's a treasure and it's always been a treasure.

"I never spoke to him directly and I never saw him directly and I never saw him face to face. [But] I knew he was a fan of the song. This was in 1987, so we didn't have email then. I'm sure I wrote him a little note that said, 'Thank you so much, let's get together.' I probably said all of that stuff but we never met in person.

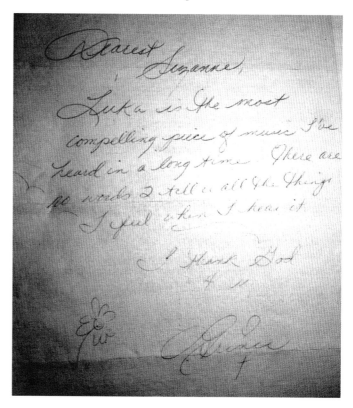

"After listening to some of his music, especially 'When Doves Cry' and after seeing *Purple Rain*," she continued, "one can imagine there was probably a lot of turbulence in his household growing up, so he probably had related to it in some way."

As Vega recounted during the 2012 tour that marked the 25th anniversary of the *Solitude Standing* album, Prince came to her July 1987 show in Minneapolis. He made a special request to come into the auditorium, inevitably surrounded by bodyguards, after everyone was seated. He sat on the flight cases at the side of the stage, got up and danced – and then, enigmatic to a fault, left the building. Suzanne never saw him.

'Luka' went on to become Vega's biggest-ever hit in America, and received three Grammy nominations including Song of the Year. It lost out in that category to 'Somewhere Out There', written by Barry Mann, Cynthia Weil and James Horner and recorded by Linda Ronstadt and James Ingram. With pleasing symmetry, the *Solitude Standing* album was released on the very same day as Prince's *Sign o' the Times*.

On March 2, 1988, at the 30th Grammy Awards at Radio City Music Hall in New York, host Billy Crystal introduced a live performance by Vega. Looking back on the low-definition clip, the entire setting seems almost unbelievably innocent, endearingly and entirely free of distracting bells and whistles. It's simply one woman and her acoustic guitar, owning the room with low-key grace.

Asked later for her most memorable Grammy memory, as a fan or nominee, Suzanne chose that performance when she said: "Singing 'Luka' by myself, without a band, and seeing Prince jump to his feet in the audience when I finished. That was a great moment for me."

On Facebook in the fateful month of April 2016, Vega posted a photograph of herself on the event's red carpet, remembering Prince's fanboy behaviour at the end of her performance. "I can't believe he's gone," she wrote.

Reflecting on her admiration for Prince as an artist and a human, Vega went on to say: "He was a music fan, and an artist in every sense of the word. When he got up in the morning and dressed himself, everything he touched and felt he put his stamp on, and you really see it in the letter. It's an expression of the man himself. It's a beautiful piece of art that you can practically feel his fingertips on."

Opposite: The letter that Prince sent to Suzanne Vega praising her 1987 hit 'Luka'.

Left: Suzanne Vega performs in March 1987 in New York City. At the 1988 Grammy Awards, Prince jumped to his feet to applaud her pared-back performance of 'Luka'.

"Singing 'Luka' by myself... and seeing Prince jump to his feet in the audience when I finished. That was a great moment for me." Suzanne Vega

CHAPTER EIGHT

THE PRINCE

AND THE MERMAID

Opposite: Prince and Mayte Garcia
perform on stage at Brabanthallen, Den
Bosch, Netherlands, in March 1995.

By the time the new millennium approached, Prince had already been all things to all people; and had even gone as far as being an acronym of himself. TAFKAP, The Artist Formerly Known As Prince, eventually came through the unpronounceable symbol years of rebellion against the perceived tyranny of his erstwhile gatekeepers at Warner Bros. That incarnation had now segued into a new life as an independent artist.

The 1996 album *Emancipation* said it all, as the star embarked on a new business model of licensing his music to companies on a one-by-one basis. EMI won the right with that release, and helped Prince tell the world about his freedom from 18 years of alleged servitude at one major label, as he formed an (albeit brief) partnership with another. They spread the word about this peculiar purple parole, even making promotional *Emancipation* sweatshirts for the media.

As the last weeks of the 1990s progressed, it became known that a new studio album – prodigiously, Prince's 23rd in 21 years – was imminent. *Rave Un2 The Joy Fantastic* had been recorded over a 15-month period at Paisley Park, as well as at New York's famed Electric Lady and O'Henry Sound Studios in Burbank, California. This time, it was Arista Records that won Prince's hand in another arranged business marriage. Celebrated music mogul Clive Davis, who had founded Arista in 1974 and navigated its decades of chart-conquering success, saw an opportunity.

Album launches in the record business have traditionally taken the form of a gentle *soirée* for journalists and other supposed media tastemakers. To be frank, we are often lured there as much by the promise of free refreshments and the chance to catch up with fellow scribes as by the prospect of being first to hear a new record. Especially

when Davis invited London-based writers to a celebration of *Rave Un2 the Joy Fantastic* a week *after* its release.

The location was the Mermaid Theater, much used in later years for live concert recordings by the BBC, including one by Glen Campbell that was to become a cherished memory. On 15 November 1999, it became the scene of something that was less a record launch than an industry seminar. Davis, standing at a lectern, spoke for what felt like days, before announcing that we were to hear the entire new Prince album, all 64 minutes of it.

That week in *The Guardian*, journalist Tom Cox captured our growing collective desperation at the event. "It was an exasperating juxtaposition of moods," he wrote. "The flashback to an evil maths teacher cackling as he informed us that the lesson would overrun well into our lunch break, battling with the suspense and uncertainty as to whether we were ever going to see The Artist perform."

But what happened next turned drudgery to delight. About two and a quarter hours after our arrival, suddenly, there on stage was the artist currently known as The Artist and his outrageously funky band, ripping into 'Let's Go Crazy'. And he did. The moment to party like it was 1999 had arrived for real.

The set played like a mini-greatest hits, including 'U Got the Look' and 'Kiss,' and a homage to heroes like Jimi Hendrix ('Red House'), Dizzy Gillespie ('Night In Tunisia') and Larry Graham from Graham Central Station and, before that, Sly and the Family Stone. More of that pivotal bassman's role in Prince's life follows in a moment.

Acutely aware of how rare Prince's London visits were, EMI had thought to invite various celebrities to join the journalistic hoi polloi, and they didn't have to ask twice. One of them later shared her experience of the occasion with me. British soul figurehead Beverley Knight was rising fast at the time. Herself signed to EMI, her major label debut *Prodigal Sista* had offered up numerous hits and was on its way to gold certification. She was *not* going to miss this one.

"Anybody in the industry who knew me knew I was Prince-crazy," she said. "I was invited along and I leapt at the chance. So I found myself in this theatre sat next to Beck, who I also love. Prince went on and tore a *hole* through the place. I loved the show. Larry Graham was on bass at the time, and he spotted me and pulled me up on stage, and Beck too.

"So there we are, dancing behind Prince, and I'm like, 'Ohmygodohmygodohmygod!' and at the end of the show, Prince's security said would you like to say hello? Of course I said I would. So I said a very brief hello to him, and I thought, 'I'm never going to wash my hands again.'"

Almost immediately, their paths intersected on a second occasion, and this time Knight would stumble upon a huge compliment from her hero. Both artists were booked for a special comeback edition of the seminal 1980s TV music show *The Tube,* taken out of mothballs by Channel 4 to celebrate the dawn of the twenty-first century. *Music of the Millennium* was headlined by Prince, Paul McCartney and Robbie Williams.

"I was in my dressing room," remembered Beverley, "and I could hear a copy of my album being absolutely *blazed*. It was down a corridor somewhere far from me, but it was that loud, I could hear it.

I thought, 'Who's that playing my album? That's so nice.' Then a few other people who were also on this big TV show came running into my room [saying], 'Prince is playing your album!' Of course, I nearly wet myself.

"I ended up in this situation where I didn't physically get to see him at that show but everybody was saying he was talking about me and he was a fan of this album, which was *Prodigal Sista*. I was just blown away." Prince's creative radar was, as always, in full working order.

Opposite: The "emancipated" Artist cuts a cool figure at Lakewood Amphitheater in Atlanta, Georgia, in 1997.

Above: Arista Records founder Clive Davis and Prince attend the *Rave Un2 The Joy Fantastic* album launch at the Equitable Center in New York, September 1999. Prince's custom-made, floor-length red tunic had a mesh fabric pattern on the chest and high slits on each side.

"[People] came running into my room [saying], 'Prince is playing your album!' Of course, I nearly wet myself." Beverley Knight

CHAPTER NINE

HATS OFF TO LARRY

Opposite: Larry Graham performs a Prince tribute at the 2016
ESSENCE Festival at the Louisiana Superdome in New Orleans.
Funkmaster Graham was a founding member of Sly and the Family
Stone and hugely admired by the young Prince, who later invited
him into his band.

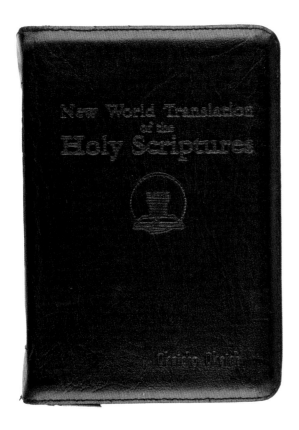

Above and below: Prince's personal travel bible, a 1984 edition of the New World Translation of the Holy Scriptures, used by the Jehovah's Witnesses church.

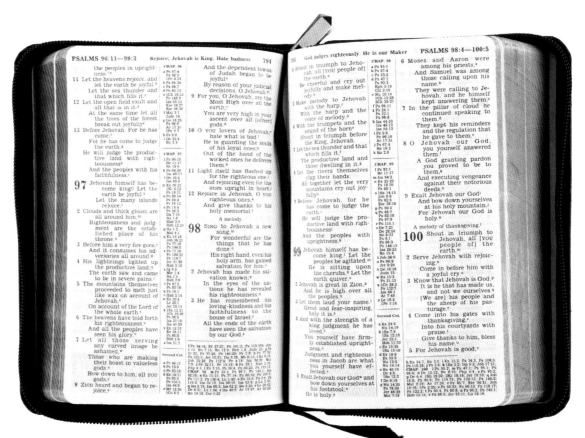

Larry Graham, creator of the groundbreaking and exhilarating slap-bass style he introduced as a member of Sly and the Family Stone, later told me the origins of his collaboration with a man who had idolized his work. Prince's first approach to him came in the late 1990s, when Graham became a compass in the younger man's personal — as well as his professional — life.

I t was Graham's faith that encouraged Prince to become a Jehovah's Witness. And because he was raised a Seventh-day Adventist, this was no whim. The friends discussed and debated the subject for two years before Prince joined the movement in 2001. "I don't see it really as a conversion," he told *The New Yorker* in 2008. "More, you know, it's a realization." "Brother Nelson" attended meetings at the Kingdom Hall in Los Angeles, once appearing, according to *The Wall Street Journal*, in a white suit and jewel-studded heels.

He also played on two of Larry's albums, and they became so close that even Graham's grandchildren came to know him as "Uncle Prince". "When I first hooked up with him," said Graham, "we were playing in Nashville. Prince was [at] the big arena there, and he heard I was in town and invited me to come down to this aftershow, his famous aftershows that he does.

"It started at about three in the morning, and when I went up on the stage, because we had met briefly at a Warner Bros picnic years before, we just exchanged greetings. But everywhere I went [musically], he was right there. It was like we'd been playing together for aeons.

"What I didn't know, and later on he told me, was that one of his biggest influences was Graham Central Station. Then he went back and listened to Sly and the Family Stone. By the time I got to Graham Central Station [circa 1973] he was older and writing and producing and doing his own thing."

Graham's wife Tina, always by his side during interviews, revealed how Prince would tell them that when he came home from school, he would play Larry's records over and over again; so much so, he would to have to buy replacement copies. "Little did I know it was going to be like that," said Larry. "We just clicked, and he said, 'What do you think about joining my tour?' I did — and that was the beginning of our friendship."

"I don't see it really as a conversion. More, you know, it's a realization."
Prince

CHAPTER TEN

HIGH ON LIFE

Opposite: If it's July 3, it must be Denver. A date at the city's McNichols Arena in 1986, as Prince's incessant live schedule and work ethic continued unabated.

Susan Rogers was among Prince's most trusted and valued insiders during her period on his A-team in the 1980s. We've heard how they went toe to toe in their feats of physical endurance and became the last two standing when all their workmates had bailed. She was one of those confidants who realized that to be in Prince's gang, you had to be available *all* the time.

"The way he worked in those days is that he was constantly recording and writing new material," she explained to me. "Many people are under the assumption that if anyone is working constant 24-hour sessions, with just a four-hour break in between, that they must be on some sort of stimulant. We used to joke about Prince that he would get high on a Coca-Cola, because he didn't take any stimulant or any drugs."

Susannah Melvoin, of The Family and later The Revolution, witnessed exactly the same phenomenon. As she looks back on it decades later, she can hardly believe what he achieved, or what he demanded. "He was so prolific," she told me, "it was nuts. 24/7. We were in Chanhassen, or it may even have been Eden Prairie. We had a warehouse and he had a studio set up in there.

"*Around the World in a Day,* The Family record, going into [the film] *Under the Cherry Moon,* the *Parade* record … he was so prolific, it didn't stop. I do have to say, it was that specific period of time from *Purple Rain* to just as the *Sign o' the Times* album was being recorded, that he was non-stop and he had the same group of us around him.

"We were great players, or I could say characters in this book – he being the author of this extraordinary book that he was writing. Unfortunately, he never finished the play, so there was no real ending for any of us as players with him. But in that period of time, he was on fire creatively, and we were right there with him."

Prince's painfully high expectations began with himself. They were ultimately informed by his soul-deep passion for music; and a boyish sense of wonder that he had earned the right to play with a huge toybox of infinite possibilities. Much-travelled music executive Alan Leeds, the artist's tour manager at his commercial peak and later president of Paisley Park Records, told *The New Yorker* in 2017: "He didn't see music as work. It's just what he did. If you called it work, you were a cynic."

But there were times when Prince would test the fortitude of those around him way beyond the point of reason. "His work ethic was crazy," says Melvoin. "If you couldn't keep up, you were out. You had to really want this, and we all did. This is something he'd say a lot: he'd call you up at three o'clock in the morning and say, 'I'm cuttin'

[recording]. What are you doing?' 'Er, sleeping?!' 'I don't know what you're doin', but I'm cuttin'!' And then he'd hang up.

"And you knew you had to be at the studio, and when you'd get there, the machine in his brain was working overtime. So there was no 'Hey, how's it going? Great to see you!' None of that. It was time to work. There were no conversations. Just, 'You're coming in to what I'm doing, do the parts, then you can leave, if I let you.'"

"For me, there's nothing like working in a recording studio," Prince

Opposite: Prince and the uncontested "Queen of Hip-Hop", Mary J. Blige, during the 2012 iHeartRadio Music Festival in Las Vegas. The duo sang 'Nothing Compares 2 U,' written by Prince and popularized by Sinéad O'Connor.

Above: Engineer, producer and audio technician Susan Rogers speaks during a panel in 2018. Rogers played an irreplaceable role in Prince's music in the 1980s and is now Professor, Music Production & Engineering at Berklee College of Music.

told *Insider* magazine as early as 1978. "It's satisfying. It's like painting. Soon, it's like the monitors are canvas. The instruments are colors on a palette, the mics and board are brushes. I just keep working it until I've got the picture."

"You were on his time schedule," says Melvoin. "Only when it was loose in rehearsal, which was again not often, he would get playful, and once he knew that the band was tight and that you were 'on' with him, then [it was] break time, and everybody would go outside and play basketball or whatever. He'd be funny and quirky, and everybody would be. But when it came to work, he wasn't the clown at all. If he was having a full conversation with you, he wasn't working.

"You'd find him [there] sometimes after the engineers had to go because their ears were bleeding. They had to work 24 hours a day, Susan Rogers and [fellow engineer] Peggy McCreary and all these people back in the day. He would be, 'OK, you can go, get yourself something to eat,' and he would be at the 24-track tape.

"He'd be splicing and cutting and you could hear him moving the wheels until you could hear that perfect drum. Then he'd cut it, put it together, get back at the board, turn the fader up, hear the edit, get back up, change something, come back, play with the faders and the EQs … it was *constant*. It was quite beautiful to watch him."

McCreary herself described how the boss's unrelenting demands

Above: Prince in action at McNichols Arena, Denver, on July 3, 1986, where he not only played Joni Mitchell's 'A Case Of You' but welcomed her on stage in person for the second encore of 'Purple Rain'.

Opposite: Prince at the Joe Louis Arena, Chicago, during the 1984–85 Purple Rain Tour, which played almost one hundred shows and sold an estimated 1.7 million tickets.

could occasionally contain unexpected benefits. "He came in one time on my birthday," she told *Pitchfork*. "I was like, 'God, couldn't he give me my birthday off? Shit!' You could always hear him walking through the courtyard because he had those high-heeled boots and he had a certain way of walking.

"But he was dressed totally different than I had ever seen him: black leather boots, jeans – which he *never* wore – white T-shirt and a black leather jacket. We cut a rockabilly song all day long. So we finished up, and I made him a cassette and handed it to him. And he stood there at the door with a little smile on his face and threw the cassette at me and said, 'Happy birthday'. And that was my birthday song. I have an unreleased Prince song."

Studio engineer, drummer and producer Justin Stanley, husband of Prince collaborator Nikka Costa, worked with him on *Hit n Run Phase Two,* the last album to be released in Prince's lifetime, in 2015. "We were almost finished with the album," Stanley told *Vibe* magazine, "and Prince tells me to set up his mic and that he would call me when he was done.

"So it's probably around six in the evening and I had left the studio. Prince calls me in the next morning. I walk into the studio and he's already recorded every lead vocal to every song on that record. It was the most amazing thing. That just blew my mind."

Admirer KT Tunstall, herself passionate when it comes to career commitment, was always in awe. "I can't quite fathom how he did what he did, physically," she observed in our 2017 interview. "He would do these massive shows and every night he'd be going off and playing three-hour aftershows in little clubs. His work ethic in the studio was pretty much 24 hours a day."

"We got calls in the middle of the night," said Susan Rogers with a laugh, "but we got calls in the middle of the day. The middle of the night for us could be 10 o'clock in the morning, because we would work all night. So you'd leave the studio after the sun had come up, take a shower, get in bed and be asleep for, who knows, two or three hours, and that phone rings. It was either Prince, or if it was during the week, someone who worked in his office. 'He needs you.'

"You'd just get out of bed, put some clothes on, get back down to that studio and keep going. I was young and there was nowhere on earth I would rather be, so when that call came, it was more sweet than bitter. It was always just a little bit funny, because you'd think to yourself, 'This is impossible. This can't be done.' And yet it can be done.

"I never saw him cancel a show due to illness. He never claimed he was sick, he never claimed exhaustion. He never didn't appear where he was supposed to be. He had a very strong work ethic, and he *always* showed up.

"He got colds and the flu, like everyone else, but he would use DayQuil or some other over-the-counter cold medicine, and he'd take the stage, he'd be in the studio, he'd do what he had to do. I think he was partly driven by his optimism and cheerful attitude and gratitude for what his life had become."

To Tunstall's regret, she never saw a full show by Prince. But one of the great landmarks of her early success was shared with her inspiration. In February 2006, when she was everyone's favourite new artist thanks to the success of her *Eye to the Telescope* album, the Scottish star had three nominations for the BRIT Awards. She performed one of the record's signature songs, 'Suddenly I See', at the ceremony and went on to win the award for British Female Solo Artist.

But just as thrillingly for her and for those of us lucky to be there, Prince was also in the building to witness her moment of glory.

"Certainly Prince had no experience of having a boss and being late for work. So he had to rely on the experiences of his staff for much of his inspiration..." Susan Rogers

He reunited with Wendy & Lisa and Sheila E. to play a seismic set including 'Te Amo Corazon' and 'Fury' as well as 'Purple Rain' and 'Let's Go Crazy'. We followed his instruction.

"It was just as special as winning a BRIT," laughed Tunstall. "He took Earls Court and turned it into this other-worldly EnormoDome, and you were transported from Earth, really. It didn't feel like you were anywhere, you were at his show."

The Scottish artist, a fireball of performance energy herself, would come to know the inside stories from workmates who served with Prince, and in particular one of his extraordinary tricks of the live music trade. "People may not know what an incredible producer, technician and engineer he was," she says. "One of my friends, [engineer] Sean Quackenbush – the man with the best surname in the world – was working on his tour.

"He was saying, and I'd heard this before, that Prince would often [use] the audience's reaction as an indicator of what his front-of-house sound was like. If you're on stage, particularly at a large gig, you've absolutely no idea what the sound is like out front. He was such a control freak and such a perfectionist, he'd be reading the audience and decide that the front-of-house sound wasn't good enough.

"The crew would have an empty flight case. That's the big box on wheels that the gear would go in, at the side of the stage. Prince would get in it, and they'd roll him with the lid on down the middle of the crowd, who'd just think it was a piece of equipment. They'd get all the way out to the sound desk in whatever arena they were in. Prince would jump out, fix the sound at the desk, jump back in the flight case and get wheeled back to the stage. In a box."

In a later chapter we'll hear backroom stories about Prince's record-busting 21 nights at London's O2 Arena. But Rob Hallett of AEG Live, who booked the shows, confirmed that the same device was used to get him on to the actual stage. "It was built with a seat in it," the promoter told me. "He'd come from the dressing room and the show was in the round, so the challenge was how to get him on stage without people seeing him.

"Every night, we'd all be standing there almost saluting him as he sat in his little box. The roadies would wheel him down the corridor to the stage. He gets on to the stage, the lights go out and, POW! the fireworks start."

Prince's bass-playing hero and later band member Larry Graham told me about an occasion in 2012, the night before he was due to fly to Europe for festival shows. His Minneapolis neighbour was on the line. "He said, 'Let's jam. Bring your bass,'" recalled Graham. Guess who?

"That always happens," laughed Larry. "By the time it was over it was time to stop. We needed to go and get ready to catch the plane."

Susan Rogers called to mind one night around 1984. "I was at home in Minneapolis, and I had a rare night off," she said. "Maybe Prince was out of town, I don't remember, but I knew I was free, and I had a date. We had a really nice time, went out to dinner, came back and we were at my place, and the phone rings. This was probably one or two in the morning. Sure enough, it was Prince.

"He was back from whatever he was doing, and he said [she adopts clipped speech]: 'Susan? Can you come to the studio? I want to record.' And that was how he spoke – it was this stern monotone. So I left, went to the studio and worked all night, and my date, who also worked for Prince, showed up at the studio late afternoon the next day. I was still there, in the same clothes. I'd been up all night.

"I spoke recently with Sal Greco, my date that night, and he remembered this story. He recalled asking me if I was going to change out of my date clothes before heading into the studio and that I said, 'No! I want him to see that I have a life!' Now, this could be a stretch of my imagination, but I seem to remember that we recorded the initial version of 'Manic Monday', to send to the Bangles, during that days-long session.

"The memory is there because I wondered if my rushing to the studio in 'going-out' clothes, and kind of dishevelled, might have planted the seed for the song. Certainly Prince had no experience with having a boss and being late for work. So he had to rely on the experiences of his staff for much of his inspiration, especially when writing from a woman's perspective."

But Rogers was not about to moan about the unexpected shift. "That was the life. I'm not complaining. It was exciting and thrilling," she continued. "Given the choice between a date and being in the studio with Prince, yeah, I'll take the studio, please. That was perfect. But it was exhausting, and not sustainable. It's not something I could do for too many years. So at a certain point, it needed to stop and real life needed to intervene." She is now a hugely revered professor at Berklee College of Music in the departments of Music Production & Engineering and Liberal Arts. Rogers is also the director of the Berklee Music Perception and Cognition Laboratory. "But every time I saw him after leaving, it was warm and happy and congenial," she said. "I'm glad that I left when I did and I treasure that he and I were able to stay on good terms."

CHAPTER ELEVEN

MEMOS FROM PAISLEY PARK

Opposite: Prince's Paisley Park Studios in Chanhassen, Minnesota, just after completion in 1988.

"A place where art, music, fashion, and culture are celebrated, energized and inspired by the visionary creative spirit of Prince." That could be a description of just about anywhere he put his small and nimble feet. But it's also the official self-description of Paisley Park, which is a 20-minute drive from the Twin Cities down Interstate 5 to 7801 Audubon Road.

The complex in Chanhassen, Minnesota, became his bolthole from 1987 onwards and, at some unspecified point, his home. It was where he lived and, as we know too well, where he died.

These days – at least until the world was forced into retreat in 2020 – the building is not only a recording studio and 12,500-square-foot sound stage, but also an active museum and shrine to its owner. But for many years, even those of us in the media could only hang on the communiqués from the front by the lucky few who'd been allowed inside its futuristic portals. This was, by now, the refuge of a man whose retreat into a private universe could make Greta Garbo seem publicity-mad.

We knew from *Around the World in a Day*'s title song that this was going to be infinitely more than the mere corporate headquarters of Paisley Park Records, the label Prince launched with the album in 1985. "There is a park that is known 4 the face it attracts," he sang on that swirling piece of Haight-Ashbury-tinted psychedelia, with backing vocals by Wendy & Lisa. This wasn't an address, he taught us, as much as a state of mind. "Paisley Park," he sang, "is in your heart."

He told *Rolling Stone* as much in a 1985 cover story. "'Paisley Park' is in everybody's heart," he said of the song. "I was trying to say something about looking inside oneself to find perfection. Perfection is in everyone."

"We built it from scratch," architect Bret Thoeny told *Billboard* magazine of the complex in 2016. Thoeny was only 23 years old when, in 1985, he was asked to come up with the radical concept of an artist's compound. "All white aluminum, metal panels on the outside to compliment the simplicity of the landscape," he said of the design. "Very few windows because recording studios don't have windows, but also because it was his place, and he wanted privacy.

Of the location, "He didn't want to do it in LA or New York," said the architect. "He wanted to do it in his hometown. Being there to creatively support and give back to his town what it gave him. I don't think he'd ever want that to change."

Prince had unveiled the song 'Paisley Park', and the full *Around the World in a Day* album, with a personal appearance at Warner Bros Records in February 1985. Arriving in a purple limousine at 45 minutes' notice, he wore an antique kimono (purple, naturally), striped pyjama-style pants and held a single pink rose. At the playback, executives applauded the LP track-by-track and stood up and cheered at the end. By then, Prince had vanished.

Six months after Prince's death, Paisley Park was thrown open to the public, notably to help the family deal with a sizeable tax bill. From the road, wrote *The New Yorker*, it looked "industrial, utilitarian and cheerless, like a big-box store that has recently gone out of business".

His ashes are now mounted above the white marble floor. But, Tardis-like, those external appearances were entirely deceptive, certainly while Prince lived there.

Mat Snow's 1992 description of the 65,000-square-foot, $10 million complex in *Q* magazine detailed an aqua blue reception area and a trophy cabinet containing sundry prizes. They included Prince's Oscar for the *Purple Rain* soundtrack, his gold record as producer of Sheila E.'s *Romance 1600* album and a State of Minnesota proclamation of Paisley Park Day.

During the building of the facility, a cat was found on-site and stayed to become a studio resident, inevitably named Paisley. Prince had his own table-tennis table, at which he would defeat Michael Jackson on a 1986 visit. One also struggles to think of another studio facility with a pair of resident doves, who lived more than comfortably in a cage in the gallery situated above the atrium. No need for *them* to cry.

Testimonials from and signed photographs of stars who had used one of its three studio facilities, from Steve Miller to Barry Manilow, decorated the space. Paisley Park's head of wardrobe, Stacia Lang, ran a department of eight staff, all tasked with styling Prince and the New Power Generation for his everyday wear and all of their stage work.

Lang advised that the colour *du jour* was citron yellow, with royal purple, red and chartreuse also approved. Studio A, meanwhile, was lined with six tons of imported, hand-cut and polished Italian marble, granite and cherry wood.

On that visit, the wardrobe director told *Q* of her vital role in Prince's meticulous appearance. "I will present him with a portfolio of 10 or 15 sketches, including for the stage a selection of sexy, lightweight garments," she said. "Just recently he wanted designs for Nehru jackets. He never wears jeans and a T-shirt, but he has to be comfortable – lots of silks and crepes.

"By day, he sticks to tailored looks but at night he wants to look as dramatic as when [he's] on stage. He loves to reveal his physique with nipped-in waistlines. Hats add drama to an outfit. He has a bowler, but his hairdos are so unique – right now it's the Typhoon – that he doesn't cover up too much. And he does love to experiment with accessories.

"We've recently had made for him some walking canes with Arabic writing down the shaft, and he loves cufflinks and his pendant with his love symbol on it." Many of his stage costumes are now on display in the museum, if such a word is appropriate.

Opposite page: Prince's Paisley Park Studios in Chanhassen, Minnesota, in 1988. The building contained a full recording studio as well as a 12,500-square foot sound stage.

Above: The outside of Paisley Park Studios, which were opened to the public after the artist's death.

Into this lair of futuristic sophistication, in 1991, stepped Alan Edwards: then, as now, one of the UK's most respected entertainment publicists, latterly as CEO of the Outside Organisation. His visit to Chanhassen was to be his initiation into Prince's private universe, and the beginning of a relationship that lasted into the twenty-first century.

"The first time I met Prince, I didn't actually meet him," Edwards told me with a laugh when we chatted about the occasion. "I got a call from his office to go out to Minneapolis, in case I was interested in doing [his] PR. Of course, I jumped on the next plane, got to Minneapolis, arrived at the airport and was met by a driver, who didn't say much.

"We got in a limo, and I remember it being winter and very flat there in Minneapolis/St Paul. Then there's this clearing in the trees, and this extraordinary futuristic building pops up, looking like something out of *E.T.*, which is Paisley Park.

"I'm taken around to the entrance, I walk in, nobody really says anything much," he went on. "I'm shown upstairs to a room which is kind of suspended. It's glass on all sides, including underneath. I'm sat in there and nobody's come in to offer me tea or coffee, or said anything to me. After about ten minutes, I'm thinking, 'This is quite odd.'

"Suddenly, music starts playing, and it's *Diamonds and Pearls.* Obviously, an incredible record, but I'm very conscious that I'm being observed in some way. It's a bit like being in Regents Park Zoo, except that I can't see where the tourists are.

"So I'm listening to the album and I thought, 'I'd better put lots of emotion into this, because that may be the difference between getting the account or not. So, lots of air guitar or whatever. Actually, it was a wonderful, special album, I didn't need to fake anything at all. I was blown away by the record.

"Anyway, the album plays and at the end of it, nothing happens, it's silent. I'm assuming someone's going to come and talk to me, or I'm going to meet Prince. Then an assistant comes upstairs and says, 'Your car's outside.' I've flown halfway around the world. I didn't say anything. I went back downstairs, got back in the limo, about half a mile back from the driver.

"Then the guy starts asking me questions. He says, 'What do you think of the album? What do you think of this track, this guitar?' And I realized I'm being very carefully pumped for my opinion. Luckily, I'd been completely knocked out by what I'd heard, so it was easy to be evangelical about the music. But I wasn't sure whether it was being relayed back to Paisley Park, or taped, or whatever.

"The guy deposited me back to the airport and I flew back to London. About three days later, I get a phone call from someone at Paisley Park saying 'You're hired if you want to do the PR.' And that was my first sort-of meeting with Prince."

Another story about a visit to the mystical headquarters says a lot about the Paisley Park owner's keen awareness of the entire pop

"It was great to see then just how much control Prince was exerting on his career..." Glenn Tilbrook

landscape. You might not have expected him to know much about a beloved British band who emerged in the late 1970s from Deptford, but it turned out that he knew about Squeeze. But then, if anyone was cool for cats, it was Prince.

Squeeze co-founder Glenn Tilbrook takes up the story. "We worked in the mid-80s with an engineer called Femi Jiya, who was really great," he recalls. "The record company took a lot of persuading that he was a good guy to work with. Then – and I'm not saying it was anything to do with us – he got the call from Prince to go and work in Minneapolis.

"We were playing there and Femi, at that point, was on a pager, and any time you got the call you had to go back to Paisley Park. So he got the call, and he invited us over, [Squeeze co-founder] Chris Difford and I. We got a full tour of the studio, and a message: 'Prince said to say he knows your stuff,' which was suitably Prince-like and enigmatic. It just made us laugh." One can't help flippantly wondering whether he preferred 'Up the Junction' or 'Take Me I'm Yours'."

Joking aside, Difford and Tilbrook's visit to Paisley Park was an insight into how to run your own affairs in the music industry. "It was great to see then just how much control Prince was exerting on his career," says Tilbrook, "and his ability to produce stuff, from videos to films to records and clothes. The whole place was a hive of industry, intensively creative and in the middle of nowhere."

American pop, soul and blues talent Nikka Costa has her own Technicolor memories of her visit to Paisley Park. First recording in 1981 at a mere nine years old, she went on to perform with Prince many times as a friend and collaborator over a 15-year period.

His ears had pricked up when Costa's 2001 album *Everybody Got Their Something* became her first to be released in the USA. He started to perform its song 'Push and Pull' in concerts the following year, and the camaraderie grew when she joined him to sing it on stage one night.

"That was amazing because I'm such a fan and he's been so cool," Costa said on MTV, remembering how she boldly told him, "'I want to write with you on my record.' He was like, 'Send me a poem.' I said, 'OK', and sent him a poem, and he came back and MP3ed me this beautiful kind of jazz thing with him singing it. It's really cool."

This page: A selection of stage accoutrements favoured by Prince and his equally well-dressed bandmates, including his chainmail cap (**Left**) and signiture heeled boots baring his logo (**Above Right**).

Opposite: The lurid colours of Prince's guitars couldn't outshine his brilliance as a player. The introduction of 'When Doves Cry' and the solo in 'Purple Rain' are two of hundreds of examples.

Left: A kick drum head from Prince's first touring band, 1979–80, with the "i" of his name signified by a tiny heart. It features in the group's TV debut on *Midnight Special* in 1980.

Below, left: In the mid-1990s, Prince often wore complete outfits dedicated to the New Power Generation, including this hockey-style jersey in purple and gold, a reference to his home town football team, the Minnesota Vikings.

Below, right: A grey scarf with chenille loop wraps worn by Prince.

Pestana Palace

★ ★ ★ ★

HOTEL & NATIONAL MONUMENT

LISBOA · PORTUGAL

TELL DAVID :
UNAUTHORIZED
PICS ON
PRINCE.ORG.COM
NEED 2 COME
DOWN . ASAP

A member of
The Leading Hotels of the World

Rua Jau. 54 · 1300-314 Lisboa · Portugal · Tel: +351 213 615 600 · Fax: +351 213 615 601

Above: The date is unknown, but the message from Prince to his lawyer is loud and clear, on paper from the Pestana Palace Hotel in Lisbon.

"It's one of my proudest moments – to have written a song with him that he wanted to record." Nikka Costa

she included her own version on the 2017 album *Nikka & Strings, Underneath and In Between,* as well as her rendition of 'Nothing Compares 2 U'. Work had started before his "transition", as she called it, but the recording took place after his departure, which made for a painfully poignant session. "The first time I met him," Costa said in my *Prince and Me* documentary, "we were invited via email to play at his birthday celebrations at Paisley Park. We went into the big space at Paisley where the bands play.

"I looked up, and on the walls were all of his outfits from every video he's ever been in. It was amazing. Then I look down and there he is, standing right in front of me. I was like, 'Oh, hi, er, hi, nice to meet you, thanks for having us.' Super-nervous, super-fumbly, super-dorky.

"Anyhow, he asked me, 'Have you ever been to Paisley before?' and I said I hadn't, and he said, 'Would you like a tour?' Of course I said yes. So Prince and I went in an elevator and walked all through Paisley Park. He showed me the offices and where he lived and told me stories about everywhere. I think we spent over an hour just chatting. I was asking him any questions, things I'd heard and read, and he was really forthright with info and advice. It was an amazing afternoon that I'll never forget."

The result was 'Silver Tongue', a bonus track on Prince's 2003 record *Xpectation.* "It's one of my proudest moments – to have written a song with him that he wanted to record," said Costa. After his death,

Above: Prince's recording archive, in which the very idea of thousands of hours of unreleased material made fans salivate.

CHAPTER TWELVE

THE PUBLIC PRINCE

Opposite: Prince performing on stage on The Ultimate
Live Experience Tour in Wembley Arena in London.
"He could spin a natural shyness as being enigmatic and
mysterious," says his 1980s collaborator Susan Rogers.

Alan Edwards's incomplete introduction to Prince's world — being whisked all the way to Paisley Park and then not meeting him — was followed by some fascinatingly odd experiences once he had landed the role of his UK publicist. His memories of one particular junket are a revealing window into his new employer's increasingly wary attitude to the media. It was a reticence that would eventually lead him to pull up the drawbridge and withhold communication almost altogether.

Back when record companies were more inclined to spend money on extravagant press trips for journalists, some of us were lucky enough to be treated to foreign adventures to cover opening nights, or to get the exclusive first interview for a major artist's new record. Sometimes, that was without even securing a commitment from our newspapers. I recall one multimillion-selling American act that always struggled for coverage in the UK, and whose record company took me to see them play in New York without any guarantee of space in the paper not once, but twice, on separate album releases.

So it was that Edwards took a posse of Fleet Street's finest on a jaunt to Rotterdam to see Prince play live. "I'd been instructed to bring out the media, about ten columnists; 3AM, Bizarre, whatever it was, not so much to review the gig but come and hang out at the party afterwards," he said. "It wasn't a particularly glamorous place, but the gig was always great.

"Afterwards, there was no sign of Prince, and I was told he was sitting down with the band and playing the show back. They were going through every single song, and everybody who'd dropped a note was going to get into trouble. Meantime, I'd gone to the club where he was rumoured to be performing one of his legendary aftershows. It's midnight, and, bit by bit, everybody's getting more drunk. One, two, three o'clock.

"I'm in touch with the bodyguard, and I'm stone-cold sober because I'm waiting for this moment … I'm thinking, 'How am I going to keep these journalists *compos mentis* in order for them to do some one-on-one chats [with him]? It gets to five in the morning, the light's beginning to come in the club, and I get the call, 'He's on the way.'

"So Prince comes, and I'm standing next to him, a few feet away, and he chats to me for about 15 minutes about who's there, what newspapers, what did they think of the gig. He never addresses a comment or question direct to me. He speaks via the bodyguard, who passes them to me, even though we're two feet away. It's a bit like

you've got a translator. Then he decided the vibe wasn't quite right and he went. That was the first time I actually met him."

But was the Howard Hughes routine a deliberate ploy? Susan Rogers has her doubts, and whether it was or not, she feels that it meant we never fully got to know the man behind the curtain. "I don't know if Prince's shyness with the media was deliberate, strategic or a happy accident," she says. "It did work in his favor, although it came at a cost. Being naturally shy is a funny form of narcissism, because it presumes that people are looking at you.

"So he could spin a natural shyness as being enigmatic and mysterious. That allowed his fans to project qualities on to him that they wanted him to have, that he may or may not have actually possessed. But the dilemma is that it prevents the artist from explaining himself. If you're not going to talk to the press, then you can't complain, and you can't explain, can you?"

Rogers, then, was one of the coterie of colleagues, if not intimates, who got to see his other side. "I don't know that the public really was aware, at least in the 80s," she muses, "of just how philanthropic he was. Or how respectful he was to women, or how he did not use profanity or pornography, or his conservative attitudes and outlook. Prince kept that quiet.

"When I was with him, I used to think to myself: 'This is going to be so remarkable, the day his story is finally told, when people finally do realize how he really is, they're going to be even more amazed.' It surprised me that he did not want his story known in those days."

Alan Edwards also told me of Prince's impish sense of humour. For all his demanding expectations of those who worked for and with him, he often had a playful smile about his lips, and the publicist enjoyed rising to his challenge.

Opposite: Prince (known at the time as TAFKAP) captured live at Brabanthallen, Den Bosch, Netherlands, in March 1995.

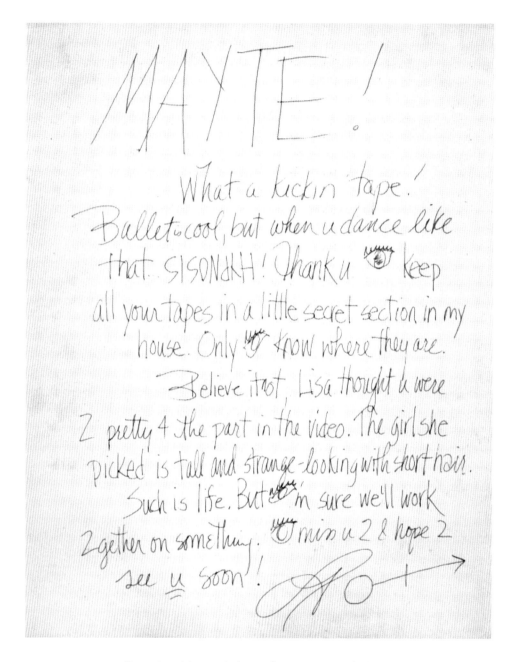

Above: An early letter to his future wife Mayte Garcia, probably circa 1989, in which he tells her that he keeps all her tapes "in a little secret section in my house".

Opposite (left): Prince during the Act I Tour at Radio City Music Hall in New York, March 25, 1993, where his set included a mere 28 songs.

Opposite (right): A few months later, in July 1993, Prince has moved on to the Act II Tour, which arrives here at the National Indoor Arena in Birmingham, England. Prince's London publicists had a "Batphone" line dedicated – and known only – to Prince for his calls.

"Our [London] office in those days was on Charlotte Street," Edwards recalled, a few months after Prince's death. "It was on the corner, in one crazy room, and my partner at the time was a man called Chris Poole. Prince was very shy, he wouldn't contemplate going through switchboards and hanging on …

"One of the provisos of the job was that we had to have a phone only for Prince. A Batphone. If it rang, it could only be Prince. So he would call up and ask things." All rather appropriate, since his 11th studio album was the 1989 soundtrack to Tim Burton's big-screen revival of the *Batman* franchise. (What was that line of the Joker's in the movie? "Haven't you ever heard of the healing power of laughter?").

"One thing I remember," Edwards recounted, "is that every month we'd get this envelope. In those days, there was no email, so we'd get this envelope in the post from Paisley Park. You'd open it, and inside there'd be 30 great transparencies … these were small pictures framed in cardboard that ended up being used in magazines.

"They'd be completely random, so it would be Prince in front of a yellow Rolls Royce, Prince in front of a purple house, Prince shopping. His instructions to us, usually, were to use whatever narrative we'd like to accompany the images. So you can imagine, as publicists, this was manna from heaven.

"The wilder the story, the better, and we would feed them to, say, Piers Morgan, or Andy Coulson, or whoever was running "Bizarre" [on *The Sun*] in those days, and of course they would exaggerate them further. Whatever figure I'd given them, say if Prince had bought a new Rolls Royce, it would immediately become a fleet of purple Rollers!" said Edwards. "So the stories would become more and more fantastic and extraordinary, and the more off the wall they were, the more Prince enjoyed them. He loved all that.

"Unlike many clients, he wasn't bothered about the minutiae in terms of what newspapers wrote. He loved wacky. He was a genius in that respect, because there was no access to Prince for the media, or anybody. But he understood the perpetual motion of his image. He really was a brilliant marketing man. Maybe Elvis was like that, I don't know, but he had that down. He was 20 or 30 years ahead of his time.

"Obviously, people like Justin Bieber handle it all brilliantly now, [and he's] as in control of his image … as Prince was. The only comparable person was David Bowie who, in a different way, understood it." Edwards speaks from experience, since he was also Bowie's long-time publicist and confidant. I once travelled with Edwards to Paris to interview the peerless chameleon for *The Times* and witnessed his similarly deft and utterly charming handling of the media.

PARTYMAN
PRINCE

THE ARMS OF ORION
PRINCE

Left: Sleeves for the 'Partyman' and 'Arms of Orion' singles from Prince's *Batman* album, for the eponymous 1989 movie starring Michael Keaton as Batman and Jack Nicholson as The Joker.

Below: The band that plays together... Prince and the New Power Generation pose on stage during the Act II Tour at Brabanthallen, Den Bosch, the Netherlands, in August 1993.

Opposite: Earlier in 1993, Prince cuts loose at his Glam Slam nightclub in Minneapolis, Minnesota.

"They were very similar in that it was theatre to both of them," said Edwards. "In a way, it wasn't real. It was an out-of-body experience. Either of those two gentlemen [could] have gone on and run Saatchi's – or any worldwide advertising agency – superbly."

The effect of being in Prince's company, he adds, was a feeling of reverence. "It was that you were in the presence of someone quite special. It was almost a spiritual reaction. It wasn't like, say, Michael Jackson where kids are screaming and jumping and running down the street. It was a sense of awe.

"And because he spoke so little and there was so little access to him – he wasn't a guy who was plastered all over the place doing big interviews – nobody quite knew how to talk to him. So everyone stood back and gave him that space, and I can't really remember a similar reaction for anyone else. Quite unique.

"When you talked to him," recalled Edwards, "normally the conversation would go [on] two or three hours, or nothing. It was one or the other. But I didn't feel any of it was affected. But eye contact, he obviously struggled with that. He was painfully shy. As much as his reclusiveness seemed like a brilliant concept, a lot of it stemmed from his shyness. He just didn't want to open himself in that way."

That was always evident from Prince's first national US press interviews. In 1980, he told the *Los Angeles Times*: "I think other people are more interesting than I am. An interview means I have to do all the talking."

"But," concluded Edwards, "he understood that he had to be visible, and he was very interested in selling the maximum number of records, being Number One and selling hundreds of thousands of tickets. He wanted to seen to be the best but on his own creative, artistic terms."

"I think other people are more interesting than I am. An interview means I have to do all the talking." Prince

CHAPTER THIRTEEN

TWENTY-ONE NIGHTS

WITH PRINCE

Opposite: Prince poses for a portrait session during his 21 Nights residency in London in 2017, when he was the talk of the capital for weeks on end.

From the moment that we learned – at a press conference on May 8, 2007 – that Prince's Earth Tour was coming to London, no one with a musical bone in their body spoke of much else. But the notion that he would be taking over London's O2 Arena for a mind-boggling 21 nights was almost too exciting for his British disciples to handle. Greenwich Prince Time was about to begin.

The commitment to a residency that would last all through August and September that year was audacious enough in itself. But all the more so since the location in question wasn't even open yet. Artists, promoters and the music business at large were still getting used to the idea that culture's whitest elephant, the former Millennium Dome, would soon, finally, be up and running as a 20,000-capacity concert hub.

The original Dome was completed in time to stand as a monument to the dawn of the twenty-first century, but to the deafening tutting of the chattering classes. Many frowned at the brain-numbing £789 million price tag, and not just those nitpickers who pointed out, not unreasonably, that we were all celebrating the new millennium a year early.

And another thing: what about that scary computer bug we'd heard about endlessly in the last months of the old decade? We were ready to party like it was no longer 1999, but what if the internet blew up and made the abacus the first essential purchase of the new dawn?

We made it, of course, but the Millennium Dome in its celebratory form was only ever supposed to be open for a year. Work on converting it into a functioning music venue started as early as 2003. Building the interior didn't begin until late 2004, and progress was so slow that many doubted whether the place would ever reopen its doors in the

name of entertainment. Then Spanish telecoms juggernaut Telefonica stepped in with a naming rights deal and the O2 Arena was born.

Soon, talks began for Prince to include the venue on his Earth Tour. One particular meeting in London, with Alan Edwards of the Outside Organisation and Rob Hallett of AEG Live (to publicize and promote the shows), gave a rare illumination of the artist's singular working methods.

"We went to the Dorchester, [because] he was staying there," remembered Edwards, already an insider from the UK promotional campaign for *Diamonds and Pearls* and from earlier London shows. "This was when we were first planning and discussing the 21 nights," added Hallett. "I think he was just sizing us up." Prince invited the executives to have dinner with him at the hotel, where he insisted on changing his outfit before meeting downstairs.

"So Rob and I have got piles of food," recalled Edwards, "and Prince has got this tiny little dish of stuff that looked a bit like dog food. I don't know what it was, it was just cereal." "He was a very finicky eater," said Hallett, "pure vegetarian. We hired a chef for him at the O2 so he had exactly what he wanted. There was nothing of him, he hardly ate at all."

After dinner and detailed discussion, the star decided that he wanted to go clubbing.

"It was about one in the morning," Edwards continued, "but he said, 'I've got to go up and change first.' So this is probably the third change, and we haven't actually gone out yet. Another costume. So we go down to Boujis, the club in South Kensington. I remember we went into the VIP room.

"Prince sat in there drinking Diet Coke or something, no alcohol, and we chatted about anything you could think of. Egyptology, the future of civilization, the internet … really interesting subjects. It was impossible to be bored in this conversation.

"At one point – we're four or five in the morning by now – I thought, 'I'd better start taking some notes, because I work for him and I should look like I'm taking all of this in. Quite how I'm going to work Egyptology into the meeting with the label tomorrow, I don't know.'

"So I started scribbling all this stuff down, but it's pitch black. I can't really see anything. At one point, he looked over my shoulder and said, 'Alan, you write just like me.' I said, 'Oh, really, what do you mean?' He said, 'Well, you write in hieroglyphics too.' I go, 'Ye-e-e-s, hieroglyphics, that's it!' Actually, I couldn't read anything I was writing, I was just scribbling to look busy. I'll never know whether he genuinely thought I was an Egyptologist, or he was taking the piss out of me. Hard to tell."

"We were asked to accompany him on several occasions," added Hallett. "Nights in Boujis, China White, and there was a club there called Hedges and Butler, which didn't close, annoyingly. You'd sit there with him and sometimes he'd be talking enthusiastically about music, the show, new acts he'd heard. Other nights you'd be sitting there in silence, staring at the walls for five hours.

"I think he was sizing us up. Alan had worked with him in the past. So we were bringing Alan back in. I remember meeting [Prince] again the next day, we were sitting there and he goes, 'I'm going to do 21 nights in London.' I went, 'Yeah, of course you are.' He said, 'I am.' I said 'P, I love you, I'm one of your biggest fans, but 21 nights, 15,000 people a night? It's a lot of people.' He goes, 'I can do it.'

"I said, 'I'll agree to the 21 nights, as long as you agree that the last seven might [have to] be in the Jazz Café. I don't know if you can do 21 O2s.' He looked me in the face and said, 'I will.' Of course I was wrong, he was right, and it was the hottest ticket in town.

"He was indefatigable," marvelled Hallett. "If you'd go out with him anywhere, it was always until six in the morning. I don't know when he slept, really, because he was up and working as well. For that period, I just dedicated my life to him, to make sure we got those 21 nights."

The May 8 press conference opened to a montage of career highlights, and then, as purple curtains parted, there was Prince himself, in sunglasses, a cream-coloured suit and a high-collared purple shirt. The Outside Organisation announced that the O2 residency, all 21 nights of it, would see him performing his greatest hits "for the very last time". For his part, he told journalists that he wanted to give his beloved UK its money's worth, since his plans afterwards would involve travelling and studying the Bible.

All tickets would be pegged at £31.21: a neat device to promote the *3121* album he'd released just over a year earlier (and the only one to debut at Number One in the USA). "Last time I was here," said Prince, "a lot of people didn't get to see me, so we're trying to make it affordable for everybody." He would, he added, live in the capital for the duration. "I love London. I've had some of my favorite shows here."

He urged people to come to multiple shows, promising constantly changing set lists from a cache of 150 songs that the media learned he had already worked up. Prince was, like all of us, falling under the spell of Amy Winehouse's *Back to Black* album, released the previous October. He said he might perform a particular favourite from it, 'Love Is a Losing Game', perhaps with Winehouse herself. That wish would come true at the last of his after-party gigs in the London run, as we'll hear shortly.

Opposite: 21 today. Prince announces his record-breaking 21-night residency at the O2 Arena in London at a press conference on May 8, 2007.

Above: A pair of tickets, otherwise known as gold dust, for Prince's The Earth Tour: 21 Nights residency at the O2, where he played to more than 350,000 people.

> ## "He was indefatigable. If you'd go out with him anywhere, it was always until six in the morning."
> Rob Hallett

Above: The former Millennium Dome opened as the O2 Arena on June 23, 2007. Prince made the place his own from August 1 to September 21.

Opposite: Amy Winehouse guested on the last of Prince's aftershows at the O2's sister venue Indigo.

The newly named O2 Arena finally launched on June 23, 2007, with an opening ceremony featuring Tom Jones, Kaiser Chiefs and Snow Patrol among others. Early residencies at the venue included those by Justin Timberlake and Barbra Streisand. The Earth Tour: 21 Nights in London extravaganza blew into town on August 1, two weeks after Prince played the Montreux Jazz Festival.

It was thanks in no small part to the indelible mark he left on the Greenwich Peninsula that, by 2008, the O2 had become the busiest concert arena anywhere around the globe. In 2009, it was named World's Best Venue by the authoritative *Pollstar* magazine.

Alan Edwards: "The band had to know 150 songs like *that*. I was privileged sometimes to sit in some rehearsals and soundchecks. He'd flick from one song to another; you'd never know which part of the catalogue he was in. I saw the drummer mess up one day. He just pushed him off and showed him how to do it.

"You'd see him at soundcheck, suddenly he's playing the keys, then he's picked up the guitar. He was a Mozart. He knew every bit of music that everyone was playing and it had to be perfect. That's what sets aside really brilliant artists, and that's why they're so rare, because most people aren't prepared [to] or capable of making that kind of commitment to their art."

Prince's opening night was a 31-song riot. He arrived on a stage shaped like his symbol imagery of old, opening with 'Purple Rain'. That first night also sported such signatures as 'Cream', 'U Got the Look', 'I Feel for You' and 'Kiss'. "You can't handle me!" he cried at one point. "I got too many hits!" The set was augmented with some impossible-to-predict covers: The Beatles' 'Come Together', Gnarls Barkley's chart-topper of the year before, 'Crazy' – and a closing blast of Chic's 'Le Freak'.

The *Guardian*'s Alexis Petridis wrote: "Quite aside from his remarkable abilities as a dancer – no mean feat given the vertiginous heels on his white boots – he milks the audience in a manner that stops just the right side of shameless." Richard Clayton's five-star ruling in *The Financial Times* concluded: "Live, this unimpeachable pop aristocrat truly has the common touch. What a regal start to his reign."

Throughout August and most of September 2007, the charismatic fireball was more than just the talking point of the English summer. You could feel him in the air, a tangible Prince among mortals and a London resident for the duration ('Build me a home by the Dome', ran a *Daily Mail* headline).

Not often during their decades of pomp had the Rolling Stones or Elton John played second fiddle to anyone; but the O2 shows they fitted into their touring schedules would feel to some like Prince's downtime. "I don't remember before or since a show creating that much excitement," says Rob Hallett. "In the press every day, Prince would be out here and there and the press loved it. The paps in London gave him a field day."

Total attendances at his O2 shows were 351,000, for an aggregate revenue of $22 million. The fact that it remains a record-breaking residency is tinged with sadness, since Michael Jackson died less than three weeks before the start of his planned 50-date stay in 2009. Each show ran to a minimum of two hours, and that's not counting the equally titanic aftershow parties at the O2's sister Indigo venue, where Prince played each night.

If the main events were testament to his prodigious flexibility in swooping and soaring amid his own catalogue and into the work of his heroes, the aftershows were like an augmented-reality tour of his record collection. As he had done at such throwdowns throughout his career, Prince's Indigo nights had him and his band busting loose on his favourites from the worlds of hip-hop, old-school soul, jazz and so much more.

"I remember one night," says Edwards, "I got back and it was a hot summer night, and I was just about falling asleep, three in the morning, the phone rings. 'Prince wants you back down here, he's going on stage at Indigo.' So I get a minicab and I'm stuck in the Edgware Road, then I get another message saying 'He's decided he's not doing it.' 'What?' And you'd go back to bed.

"He was doing fan club shows too. There were days where he was doing three shows in a day, proper shows. A fan club gig at lunchtime, a soundcheck, the show and then the Indigo. So in reality, he was playing around the clock. The stamina, for him and anyone working for him … incredible. It's mind-boggling. Now there's no one who would even contemplate it. Most artists are fussing if they've got to do three or four gigs a week. This is a guy doing three or four gigs a day."

On the first aftershow alone, he and the band tucked into A Tribe Called Quest's 'Can I Kick It' and tracks by jazz overlords Wayne Shorter and Billy Cobham. There were salutes, too, to the pioneer who was soul's godfather and Prince's forefather, James Brown, via tunes from the sax player they shared – the peerless Maceo Parker – and with the funk standard 'Pass The Peas', first cut by Brown's own crack band of the 1970s, the JB's.

Subsequent after-hours parties showed the frontman's fluency in the work of groups and soloists who schooled his musical maturation.

They included such royalty as Stevie Wonder, Aretha Franklin and Sly and the Family Stone and the less appreciated War, Rufus, the Ohio Players, Billy Preston, Tower of Power and Mother's Finest. It was a fantasy jukebox that played one perfect selection after another.

British soul exemplar Beverley Knight remembers those occasions as more than just an eyewitness. She was picked out by Prince both to open for one of the "regular" shows – has ever an adjective been less adequate? – and to perform at one of the late-night parties. Both nods were eloquent testimonial to Knight's reputation earned, by then, in a dozen years of prominence as one of Britain's most vibrant performers of any musical stripe.

We've learned elsewhere of Beverley's backstory with her idol, as an early-adopter fangirl and then at live events in the closing weeks of the old millennium. But what happened next was a screen-grab right out of her dreams.

"I was asked quite out of the blue in 2007 if I would like to open for Prince," she told me. "I'd already bought tickets to a few of the shows. I had the privilege of seeing him soundcheck. My band were laughing at me because I was standing there staring at him. I didn't realize I was gripping on to the chair in front of me like my life depended on it.

"I went on, did my performance, and it was one Prince fan to a sold-out O2 of Prince fans. So I was … in a sense, I was one of those people. There was a real synergy. I came off-stage, and to my delight, Prince's band were there, applauding me and the band off. I made my way to the dressing room, and as I was walking down the corridor, I felt this hand grab my arm pretty firmly and spin me around. And there I was, face to face with Prince.

"Of course, I had to retain composure, which wasn't easy for me, and he said, 'I want you to do my aftershow tonight, will you do it?' And I nodded. I just about managed to get the word 'yes' out. So I watched his show, which was like two and a half hours, excited beyond belief, knowing I was going to do the aftershow around the corner [inside the O2 Arena complex] at the Indigo."

Then the whole experience truly hit the clouds. "My band and I got on stage, and we were in the hands of Prince and his crew," Knight goes on. "It was absolutely rammed. My boyfriend at the time, now my husband, and his sister and his brother were there. I was obviously in heaven. I did an opening slot, and we were just jamming. I was playing my song 'Keep This Fire Burning' and Reidy, my guitarist [and musical director, Paul Reid] was just in the pocket of the groove, and we were loving our lives.

"As I was singing and ad libbing, I can hear this other guitar. I'm looking at Reidy thinking, 'That's not him, he's holding down rhythm guitar. This person is playing more of a lead style. I've got one guitarist. Who the hell is that?' I looked to my right, into the wings. Oh my god. Prince is playing along to 'Keep This Fire Burning'. Then he walks out, and of course, you can imagine. The place exploded. I'm like, is this real? I'm on stage playing my song with my band and Prince is accompanying me! This is not happening!

"I'm trying to sing and hold it together, and the tears are coming, but I'm so happy. Then, one by one, the rest of his band joined and it turned into this seamless switchover of my band into Prince's band. It was like the faders came down on us and came up on his band. I can't describe it any better than that. Down to my drummer leaving and Cora [Coleman-Dunham], who was drumming for him at the time, holding it down. It was spectacular.

"That was the first of four aftershows I ended up doing, each of them lasting a good three and a half hours. I had to take off my shoes, I was that shredded. The last one was with the late, great Amy Winehouse – myself and Amy guesting with Prince at the final aftershow, which was incredibly special." That night, he was granted the wish he had expressed at that press conference four months earlier: to host Amy's performance of her own spellbinding 'Love Is a Losing Game'.

You had to be there, of course, but the later release of the limited edition *Indigo Nights* CD, solely as part of the 2008 coffee table book *21 Nights*, provided a priceless chance to eavesdrop. Doubtless for copyright reasons, it didn't include the Prince and Amy moment; but it did offer other exquisite highlights of those unforgettable aftershows; such as a typically fearless version of Led Zeppelin's 'Whole Lotta Love' and a smooth soul take on Dorothy Moore's 1970s ballad 'Misty Blue'.

Perhaps best of all, the disc included Knight and Prince's magnificent takeover of Aretha's 'Rock Steady'. Live recordings can sometimes struggle to capture the mood of the night, but sweat drips from the CD. To coin a phrase, if it don't turn you on, you ain't got no switches. Next, Beverley will explain how she would have the chance to relive that moment in an even more unbelievable setting.

CHAPTER FOURTEEN

PRINCE'S AWARD (K)NIGHT

Opposite: Beverley Knight, British soul
favourite, lifelong fan and later collaborator with
Prince. "I got to touch greatness," she says.

British soul mainstay Beverley Knight has described many of the ways in which Prince touched her life, both as a lifelong fan and then, to her amazement, as a collaborator. Singing with him at his O2 Arena residency felt like a treat that couldn't be topped. With 14 UK Top 40 hits already to her name, including such signatures as 'Shoulda Woulda Coulda', 'Greatest Day' and 'Come As You Are', she was soon in for the surprise of her life.

"**A**s if the O2 wasn't enough," she remembered, "the February of the following year, 2008, I'm just chilling at home and I get this phone call. I hear this woman saying, 'Hi, my name's Cathy, I work with Prince, and he wants you to come to Los Angeles this weekend.' It was Tuesday!

"I'm thinking this is a complete wind-up, because it's on a mobile phone. She gives me a number, and it's a Minneapolis number. This is actually real. So I hang up the phone, I'm straight on the phone to my managers, 'Oh my god, I've just been called, what do I do?' They were like, 'What do you mean what do you do? You go!'

"So I found myself flying to LA, and I didn't actually know why I was going," Beverley continued. "The penny dropped that it was the Oscars weekend, because the hotel where he put me up was the Beverly Hills Hotel, and half of Hollywood was there. In my excitement, I just had neglected to do a bit of homework and think there might be a bigger reason why I'm here, and that reason was the Oscars.

"Prince had said that he just wanted to have a meet and a chat. Well, we did more than just meet and chat. He threw an Oscars party at his rented house up in Beverly Hills, so this is in his living room, as it were, with a temporary stage set up. And he got me on stage to sing.

"It was the most incredible thing that's ever happened to me in my musical career. I was on stage with the band, there was no set list, and that's typical of what Prince would do. Luckily, I know his back catalogue like I know myself, so wherever he was going, I was joining in.

"There was myself, Shelby J, Miss Jones – we were like the little background section – and Prince was there. I'm looking out and seeing Spike Lee, Wesley Snipes, Dave Chappelle, Chris Tucker, Javier Bardem and the Coen brothers, who still had their Oscars in their hands. Kate Beckinsale was there and came over to say hello. I was like, 'You don't know me from a tree, but hi!'

"As the show's going on, I'm thinking, 'Nothing can get any better than this.' Then I see the crowd parting, and a man being led through by another man. It's a big, burly security guy and someone I can't quite make out. As the crowd's parting, this guy's getting closer. I'm like, 'OK, this is beyond surreal. That's Stevie Wonder.' My manager was

in the crowd in complete floods of tears, he can't believe it's happening himself.

"So I'm on the right hand of the stage, and Stevie goes over to the left, where of course Prince's keyboard player has just moved out of the way slightly. Stevie gets behind the keys, and we go into a whole section of his songs. Prince is on guitar, Stevie is on the keyboard, he switches the sound to clavichord and we go into 'Superstition'. I'm thinking, 'If I die right now, my life has been incredible.'

"As the jam continues, Prince shuffles back, doesn't drop a note, whispers in my ear and says, 'I want you to sing.' I'm like, 'OK', and he says 'Rock Steady', get ready.' 'Rock Steady' [Aretha Franklin's R&B Top 10 gem of 1971] is what I sang with Prince at the aftershow at the Indigo a few months previously.

"He goes into the familiar groove, I take the mic and so I'm now singing 'Rock Steady' and Stevie's on keys. Prince is on guitar and Javier Bardem is in the crowd, the Coen brothers with their Oscars. And there's me, this kid from Wolverhampton, singing to the great and good of Hollywood. And all I can do now is laugh."

> ## "There's me, this kid from Wolverhampton, singing to the great and good of Hollywood. And all I can do now is laugh." Beverley Knight

CHAPTER FIFTEEN

DOWN ON THE FARM

Opposite: Prince gives a dynamite performance at the only
British festival he ever played, Hop Farm in Kent, in 2011.

If Prince's 2011 appearance in a field near Tunbridge Wells was unlikely, then the circumstances that got him there were positively fanciful. The occasion provides another lesser-known anecdote in his treasury of tales. It's also the answer to the trivia question about the only British festival he ever played; and it wasn't Glastonbury, V, the Isle of Wight or any others you might have expected.

That spring, it emerged that Prince was in the market to play a summer event in the UK. The opportunity arose in the wake of his 35th studio album *20Ten,* during his Welcome 2 America: Europe 2011 Tour. Vince Power, the venue and festival owner who had made his name as the founder of London venue the Mean Fiddler, was in the fourth year of his independent Hop Farm Festival, held at a country farm in Paddock Wood, Kent.

The event started modestly as a one-dayer in 2008, but served notice of its credibility by securing Neil Young as that year's headline act. By the next year, it had broadened its scope to two days, with headliners the Fratellis and Paul Weller. A 2010 line-up featuring Bob Dylan, Van Morrison, Blondie and Ray Davies amplified the message that the Hop Farm meant business.

Gill Tee was the co-founder of events company Entertee, and had made her reputation during a long tenure at London's Capital Radio, whose Party in the Park extravaganza she oversaw. Now she and business partner Deb Shilling were running their own company, and Tee was Power's right hand as Festival Director of Hop Farm.

In the later 2010s, Tee and Shilling would turn their skills to the creation of the Black Deer Festival, a celebration of Americana music and culture that quickly became one of the UK's favourite new annual gatherings. But at the beginning of the decade, Tee had other things on her mind.

"I was in the office when Vince got the call to ask if he wanted to bid for Prince," she recalled. "He'd never done a UK festival, so it was quite a big moment. We had ten weeks to go [before the July event], and two days were already doing really well, with the Eagles and Morrissey headlining. We had the ability to do three, but we'd only ever done two and the only day Prince could do was the Sunday.

"This was like a lifetime ambition for Vince, to get Prince," she continued. "It was a conversation he'd had a while back, but it had gone away. Suddenly Prince was available, and Vince ended up bidding. Hop Farm wasn't sponsored; it was privately owned, it wasn't corporate. We'd had Neil Young playing there, and Bob Dylan, so it had a good pedigree. Anyway, we ended up getting Prince." Power's famously persuasive patter had done the trick.

"I started looking at Prince around October/November," the entrepreneur told *Access All Areas* magazine of his initial bid. "[His people] were interested, but nothing happened. So I increased the offer, they found out a bit about the Hop Farm, seemed to like the vibe of the whole thing, and it went back and forwards. In the end, I think the timing was right. If he hasn't got a full plan to tour, festivals are easier obviously, all the infrastructure's there. The money helped as well."

Now it was down to logistics, as Tee recalled: "I then had to deal with the police and the council to get them to approve everything. A whole new line-up had to be found [for the Sunday bill], and we had

to promote it. I lived relatively near, and people were looking at the posters and saying, 'That can't be the real Prince!' By then, we had nine weeks to sell it."

By the weekend of Hop Farm 2011, a full Sunday bill had been added, with a main stage bill also featuring Tinie Tempah and Prince's long-time friend and inspiration, Larry Graham. Prince had just played three shows in Paris and, on the Saturday night, was at the Heineken Open'er Festival in Gdynia, Poland, travelling through the night to Kent.

All seemed set fair, until Tee received a late request for his "rider". The infamous set of backstage conditions and comforts that a major artist can demand, within their contractual agreement, is often a source of amusement or outrage. This one provided a distinct challenge.

"For his 'green room', one part of the rider had been missed off," said Tee. "They wanted a purple throne with velvet lining for his Portacabin. He wanted an ornate chair, fit for a prince! This was literally on the Saturday morning. Whether it was his

Opposite: Prince on the main stage of the Hop Farm Festival. "Suddenly he was available, and we ended up getting him," says event director Gill Tee.

Above: Prince's Hop Farm set list included covers of Michael Jackson's 'Don't Stop 'Til You Get Enough' and Wild Cherry's 'Play That Funky Music'. He told the crowd: "Parties are supposed to go on 'til everyone's asleep."

Right: An autographed set list and guitar picks given by Prince to the crew.

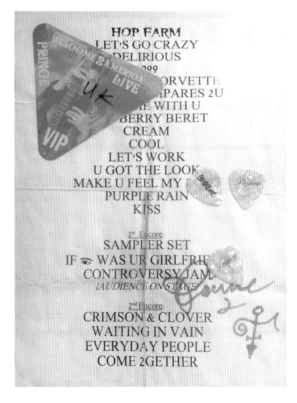

HOP FARM
LET'S GO CRAZY
DELIRIOUS
399
ORVETTE
PARES 2U
E WITH U
BERRY BERET
CREAM
COOL
LET'S WORK
U GOT THE LOOK
MAKE U FEEL MY
PURPLE RAIN
KISS

1ˢᵗ Encore:
SAMPLER SET
IF ☞ WAS UR GIRLFRIE
CONTROVERSY JAM
(AUDIENCE ON STAGE)

2ⁿᵈ Encore:
CRIMSON & CLOVER
WAITING IN VAIN
EVERYDAY PEOPLE
COME 2GETHER

entourage that demands these things, you never know. But it had to be lined with the material and look a certain way.

"So on the Saturday morning, I'm thinking, 'Where the **** am I going to find a velvet throne?' Luckily I had a friend not a million miles away who had a lapdancing club. I phoned him and said, 'I know this sounds like a very bizarre question, but you haven't got a velvet chair that looks like a throne, have you?' And he had! It was dark red, ornate, velvet, not quite purple, but close enough.

"So Saturday afternoon, my crew went to this lapdancing club and picked up this chair. It was perfect. God knows what had happened on it the night before, or what Prince would have thought if he'd known. Anyway, there it was, in the room, ready for him to turn up."

An extremely happy ending ensued. Prince and the band opened with 'We Live (2 Get Funky)' – an unreleased track they performed occasionally that year – at the outset of a two-hour orgy of energy. The big guns were out: 'Let's Go Crazy', '1999', 'Little Red Corvette', 'Cream', 'U Got the Look', 'Kiss', even 'Nothing Compares 2 U'.

The outrageous covers were there too, from Michael Jackson's 'Don't Stop 'Til You Get Enough' to Wild Cherry's 'Play That Funky Music'. When Graham joined them for the encore, it was inevitable that Prince was going to lead him back to Sly and the Family Stone territory for 'Everyday People' and 'I Want to Take You Higher', sandwiched by The Beatles' 'Come Together'. The last word was 'Baby I'm a Star.'

"I wish there wasn't no such thing as a curfew," said Prince as his enforced finale approached. "Parties are supposed to go on till everyone's asleep."

"Because you're running it, you [usually] don't get to see the show," said Tee. "You have these Safety Advisory Group meetings that have to happen every hour. So I was in this meeting and I heard him strike up 'Purple Rain'. I said 'Guys, I'm sorry, I'm out of here.'

"I put my coat on, and I could have gone anywhere, on-stage … but I walked to the back of the audience. I pulled my coat tight, I was there on my own, and I bawled my eyes out. Then all the purple ticker tape came down. It was absolutely magical. If you saw the enjoyment on his face from that audience … people who'd seen him 20 times said that performance would sit with them forever. He was incredible."

One fan wrote a post on the official message board in which he said: "For me, this was by far the best concert of recent years. Up there with the final night at the O2 in 2007. The sound was brilliant, and Prince himself seemed to be having a blast. Well done Hop Farm."

"He was very humble," said Tee of their meeting. "My technical production manager's son was on the sidelines and Prince signed a poster for him. He gave us some plectrums, and he was just nice. There was a twinkle in his eye. I think he had a great time.

"I saw [Glastonbury Festival founder] Michael Eavis at a party and he said, 'Hop Farm Festival, Gill Tee … I can't believe I was outbid for Prince. I always wanted him for Glastonbury.'

"It's even more of a highlight now that he's gone."

Above: Prince accepts applause from the crowd at the Hop Farm Festival.

Opposite: Welcome 2 Europe. Prince on the tour of that name at Rotterdam's Ahoy Stadium on July 8, 2011, the week after the Hop Farm performance.

CHAPTER SIXTEEN

A 2020 VISION

Opposite: For a television audience estimated at 140 million, Prince plays the Super Bowl XLI half-time show in Miami, 2007. Amid his own hits, covers included 'We Will Rock You,' 'Proud Mary' and 'All Along The Watchtower'.

127

While bringing this narrative to a conclusion, I was given the treat of a new conversation with "St. Paul" Peterson, whose place in Prince's world has been considerably less reported than that of other alumni.

Part of a sophisticated dynasty that's often reverently described as "Minnesota's first family of music", he became a latter-day member of the band the superstar created in the early 1980s, The Time. Dubbed "St. Paul" by Prince (after Minneapolis's "twin" city of the same name), Paul Peterson featured with them in *Purple Rain* [the movie], before becoming a member of the purple paymaster's next concept, The Family.

As the first signing to Paisley Park Records after Prince himself, that group made just one album and played just one gig, but left a distinctive imprint and set a template for the label. It helped subsequent releases by Sheila E., Madhouse, Jill Jones, Taja Sevelle and so many others to critical and, in some cases, commercial embrace.

The website Vinyl Me, Please [www.vinylmeplease.com] chose *The Family* among the ten best "Prince protégé" albums" to own on vinyl, which I'm pleased to say I do. It described the disc as "the missing link between the insular neo-psychedelia of 1985's *Around the World in a Day* and the kaleidoscopic, jazz-inflected sophistifunk of 1986's *Parade*.

"Saxophonist Eric Leeds, soon to join the expanded Revolution, enables Prince's burgeoning interest in jazz music; while [Douglas] Clare Fischer's majestic string arrangements add a touch of old Hollywood glamour to minor classics like 'The Screams of Passion' and the original version of 'Nothing Compares 2 U'."

After that album, Peterson left The Family – abruptly, as we'll hear – to pursue his own career, returning to Prince's orbit when Paisley Park was fully functioning as a studio. He has since amassed a weighty resumé of credits, playing and touring with scores of A-listers from Peter Frampton to Steve Miller and from George Benson to Glen Campbell. In 2020, as he continued work at home in Minneapolis on an upcoming solo record, his remembrances revealed much about his former boss's personality both as a label head and as a man.

"I was asked to audition for The Time when Jimmy Jam, Monte Moir and Terry Harris left – or should I say Jimmy and Terry got fired," Peterson told me. "I'd just graduated from high school and I was on vacation up in northern Minnesota. I got a call from my brother-in-law, Stewart Pastor, who is first cousins with David and Bobby Z, who are obviously Prince family.

"There was an opening for a keyboard player in The Time, and I'd been playing with Stewart in a local band with my sister during high school. He called me and said, 'Get your butt home', so I did, I came home early from my vacation. I was supposed to learn at least half a dozen songs, so I was expecting to have a cassette tape waiting for me, which did not happen.

"The deal is, I got the tape the night before the audition, so I had to learn how to play the songs, memorize them and be able to attempt to dance at the same time and act as cool as I could."

A memorable meeting was imminent, Peterson recalled his 17-year-old self feeling. "So I went into this audition, and Prince was not there; [The Time's] Jesse Johnson was. Evidently I did OK, so I got a call back. And the second day I went back, Prince *was* there. I played, and then he came up to me, and I was a little intimidated, as you might imagine.

"The first thing he did was, he wrote on a piece of paper the three words 'wreck a stow'. Like he did in the movie [*Under the Cherry Moon*], but he did it for real to me – as our icebreaker, our first encounter. He said, 'What does it say?' I said, 'Wreck a stow? I don't know!' and I'm scared to death. Long story short, we get to the point

Opposite: Prince guests on Fox TV's *American Idol* finale of 2006, accompanied by dancers Maya and Nandy McClean, the sisters he affectionately called "The Twinz".

Above: On a rainy night in Miami, the superstar plays the 2007 Super Bowl half-time show. The performance, on a large, central stage shaped like Prince's unique logo, is regarded as one of the greatest half-time shows in history.

> "Everything he touched turned to gold. He didn't have time to cultivate a damn thing." St. Paul Peterson

Above: R&B aggregation and Prince protegés The Time on *American Bandstand* in 1983 in Los Angeles.

Below: Jimmy Jam, Jellybean Johnson and The Time at the 62nd Annual Grammy Awards on January 28, 2020.

Opposite: Prince at the 2010 BET Awards, where Chaka Khan presented him with a Lifetime Achievement Award.

where he says, 'Say it fast' and I say, 'Rec-a-sto' and he says, 'Where do you buy your records?' Ah, the *record sto*'!

"Immediately following that, we went over to a bunch of swatches of clothing to pick out a suit for me for the movie *Purple Rain*. I picked out a beautiful pinstripe black suit and he said, 'You'll never get noticed in that.' He picked me out an *orange* pinstripe suit that you see me in on the cover of *Ice Cream Castles* [The Time's 1984 album]. So that was my first encounter with Prince."

The story chimes with another recounted to me by Tommy Barbarella, keyboard player in the New Power Generation for five years from the early 1990s. He had his own first-hand experience of Prince's fashion sense. It concerned the one and only song among his 40 UK hits to go to Number One, 'The Most Beautiful Girl in the World,' from his years as TAFKAP (the Artist Formerly Known as Prince). The segue is further smoothed by the fact that the chart-topper was co-produced by Paul's older brother, Ricky Peterson.

"I remember shooting that video," said Barbarella, "and Prince didn't like what the wardrobe people had put me in. He said, 'Come up here'; so I went up to his office and he had all this clothes that he was going to choose from for the video. He said, 'Try this on.'

"So I put on one of his jackets, and it was a little snug but I was quite thin at the time. Not as small as him. He was like, 'Yeah, wear that.' So I ended up wearing his clothes in that video. He liked it so much, they ended up making the same outfit for me, in my size, which was more comfortable."

Those close-knit connections were always apparent, but sometimes they concealed challenges of their own, as St. Paul explained. "Between Stuart and Bobby and David, and Robbie Pastor taking care of Prince as his valet for a long time, it was like family," he said. "But more family on the outside than it was on the inside. The *group* The Family I had to get to know, with the exception of Jellybean [Johnson] and

Jerome [Benton], who I knew from The Time, of course."

When *The Family* came out in the summer of 1985, giving rise to the Top 10 R&B hit 'Screams of Passion,' production credits were given to David Z and The Family. Prince's name was only to be seen as the composer of 'Nothing Compares 2 U'. In reality, the entire record was of his making, as Peterson confirmed.

"He probably wanted it to appear [like] it was a real band, meaning that we had got together under our own motion and had our own idea of what the band should be and that we weren't relying totally on Prince. Which is exactly what we were doing – because during that period of time, he was so prolific, and everything he touched turned to gold. He didn't have time to cultivate a damn thing.

"[But] he played all the instruments, did all the arrangements, wrote all the songs. He put together the band the way it should be and he did all the casting of characters – and, for that matter, the wardrobe. He also had me sing pretty much phrase-by-phase like he did, because he didn't have time to sit there and coddle me through that.

"However, David Z, hearkening back to the *real* family, he was the one who took me through that whole process. Prince had the vision, but when you're on fire like that, you can't dedicate years of your life to cultivate a band. That's my opinion."

When it came to Peterson's personal relationship with Prince, there were ups, downs and a happier conclusion. But, just the way we want to believe it, there was *always* that aura.

"Oh, for sure," said St. Paul. "His presence was larger than life. Others had a different relationship with him than I did, [which was] much more of an employer-employee relationship; even though I know he respected me and he certainly respected my talent, otherwise I wouldn't have been there, right?

"But he and I didn't get ultra-tight like he and Susannah [Melvoin] or he and his band members did. Because again, during that period of time, he was busy being Prince, and doing his own thing. I was there, I did the job I was asked to do to the best of my ability, and he was pleased.

"I think part of the reason I left was that he *was* absent," mused Peterson. "I couldn't turn to him and go 'Look, dude, this is what's going on, this is the problem.' When I did get a chance to say that he would just pass it on to his managers, who in turn told me 'There are no [contract] negotiations, you're either in or you're out.' And I went, 'Well, OK then, bye!'"

Yet there were times, both in the early days and much later, when Prince would show warmth to his fellow musician. "I actually lived in his house in LA with him," St. Paul revealed. "He let me stay in his father's room in his mansion, and we would get together and shoot pool. I remember specifically saying something about my relationship with Jesse Johnson and he said, 'Well, I'm not Jesse,' meaning he was opening up to me about being approachable.

"We did get along, and I remember really clearly two different times when he showed his emotion towards me. One of them was right after I got off the stage from [The Family's] one and only gig at First Avenue [the Minneapolis venue that describes itself as 'your downtown danceteria since 1970']. He grabbed me and hugged me and told me what a great job I did, which was pretty special to me.

"Then the last time I saw him was when he asked Eric Leeds and myself, with our band LP Music, to play for his album release party in

the fall of 2015. He and I had been cool for quite a period of time at that point, but he gave me a big hug and said, 'Thank you for being here, it's great to have you.'"

After his original departure from The Family, Peterson had come back into the fold, if somewhat remotely, when his brother Ricky was hired as Prince's staff producer at Paisley Park. Thereby occurred another telling and startling encounter. "Me being the little brother, I tagged along with him, and would write a lot of music and play on those acts that Prince signed," said St. Paul. "If Prince didn't like me, you know I would have been bounced out of that building.

"But we were not speaking at that point, so it was weird. He tolerated my presence and me playing on the records, but when Prince would see me in the hallway, he would immediately do a 180 and walk the other way. It was hilarious! [When] Ricky's position came to a close, I wrote Prince a note saying, 'I realize you and I have not been on the greatest of terms since I left the Family, but I want you to know I appreciate everything you've done for me, and for my family.'

"It was me clearing the air, having everything come to an end. It was a cleansing thing for me. The next day, I got a call from his people saying 'Prince wants to see you', and I'm thinking, 'I'm trying to leave but they keep dragging me back … '

"So I went up for this meeting with him, and sat in his apartment for probably half an hour. That's his psychology, to let me stew a little bit. Then he came in and said, 'Do you make a living in the music

Opposite: Football superfans were distracted from the game, as Prince owned the Super Bowl half-time with a definitive and spectacular 12-minute show.

Above: Rain-soaked fans were given a rendition of 'Purple Rain'.

Above: Prince told the crowd at the 2010 BET Awards, "I was pretty wild in my younger days."

Below: Prince performs at the 2006 opening of his 3121 nightclub at the Rio Hotel & Casino in Las Vegas.

business?' I said, 'Well, yeah.' He said, 'What do you do?' I said, 'Well, I've been here, writing, producing, placing songs and playing on your people's records.'

"He said, 'Do you want to join my band?' I said, 'What? Do tell.' He said, 'Well, if you do, it's going to be an all-meatless band, a vegetarian band." Peterson recalls the bovine infection that threatened the beef industry in the mid-1990s. "Remember mad cow disease? That's when this was happening. I said, 'No, man, I'm not doing that.'

"That was the point where we laughed a little bit. It was the breaking of the old shackles of us not getting along. I politely declined, and he said, '[that] Michael Bland [the NPG drummer] said, 'Let's discuss it over a big steak somewhere.' [I said,] 'That's where I'm at too, brother.'"

The weeks, months and years after Prince's death overflowed with every type of tribute tour and reunion you could imagine. But in 2018, St. Paul had a chance to direct, and to star in, a unique homage to the man he knew, as the musical director and frontman of the show *Nothing Compares 2 Prince*, which featured many fellow travellers and sold out two nights at the Sydney Opera House.

"I've done a lot of touring in Australia myself, and my manager Neil Richards is an Aussie," said Peterson. "Two years before this was even happening, these producers who do a lot of shows throughout Australia asked me if I would be interested in doing something like that, organizing it. When it finally came to fruition, I had such a good time putting that together.

"It was a huge undertaking, just to get the songs and the right people singing the right things. My biggest thing was, 'Look, I just

want people to come here with the right intentions and the right attitude. I don't want any divas, male or female. That's now how I operate. The bottom line is, let's celebrate this man and his music and our contribution to how we were a part of this.'

"Everyone was great," he added. "I couldn't have asked for a better crew. A lot of us didn't know each other, because, let's face it, I came from a generation before a lot of these younger folks. But the thing that bonded us together was that same education we got from Prince, it just happened to be at different times. We knew the work ethic, we knew the parts, we knew how we needed to show up and execute that show, and we did it, and I'm super-proud of it."

Naturally, the show featured the song that Peterson and The Family had helped to introduce all of 33 years earlier, 'Nothing Compares 2 U'. He performed it as a duet with Shelby J, the protégée who sang with Prince for many of his latter years. "Instead of pulling a diva moment," he laughed, "I said, 'Let me share this with Shelby, who's been singing it with him for the last few years prior to his death.'

"She had not sung it with anybody but Prince up to that point, so it was a special moment in the show and I'm glad I could share it with her. I didn't want to be a ball hog on that one."

Peterson and I joked about the fact that if the assembled cast had put a foot wrong, they would have heard about it in no uncertain terms from the Prince online community, who never miss a beat and who protect his legacy with proprietorial zeal.

"They are a special group," he noted with some understatement. "I will say, they've been very supportive of everything that I've done. I'm on the outskirts of The Revolution, The Time, NPG, all those different factions. I'm kind of my own island, which I think is a good place for me to be."

As he looks back, Peterson's sadness is at least leavened by a note of positivity. "Throughout the last few years of his life, we were hanging out," he said. "We had one meeting at the Dakota [venue] seeing Victor Wooten [bassist, producer and five-time Grammy winner]. We sat talking over his entire concert, which was strange and lovely all at the same time. We had very many great conversations over the last few years of his life."

In addition to his extensive touring with others, St. Paul's other recent work has included singles such as 'Minne Forget Me Not', a love song to Minneapolis adapted from Daryl Hall & John Oates's tribute to their home town, 'Philly Forget Me Not'. He also hosts his own regular, highly absorbing podcast series Music on the Run, in which he shoots the breeze with musicians and friends that he's toured with, from Steve Miller to Donny Osmond, about life on the road.

But he knows full well how the first line of his musical resumé will always read. "It's funny what people will remember you for," he mused. "Some people are fortunate enough to have an iconic moment in their career, even though they may have done other things that are just as important to them.

"I'm just as proud of playing with my family, or with George Benson or Kenny Loggins, those kinds of people, and I had a much longer tenure with Kenny or with Oleta Adams, and musically they were super-satisfying. But because of the iconic presence that Prince was, and is, I'll always be associated with my time with him. I think that's pretty cool."

CHAPTER SEVENTEEN

PURPLE IN PERPETUITY

Opposite: It's later than you think. Prince and his band at Warner Theater on June 14, 2015, in Washington, DC, as part of that year's Hit 'N' Run Tour.

137

"I'm gonna stop this soon," Prince once said. It wasn't a late-career declaration, but came way back in an interview with *Melody Maker* in 1981. "I don't expect to make many more records for the simple reason that I wanna see my life change. I wanna be there when it changes, I don't wanna just be doing what's expected of me. I just wanna live … until it's time to die."

As we know all too well, that desperately sad event took place long before it was time. In the closing eulogies of those insiders to whom I spoke for the *Prince and Me* radio documentary, their raw sorrow so soon after his passing was evident. They spoke of if onlys and might have beens; but still about their gratitude at being part of his life.

André Cymone was making his formidable *1969* album when his old friend and room-mate departed. "I was really looking forward to playing this new album to Prince," he told me. "It's what we did, when we were kids, and when we grew up. I actually wanted to see if I could get him to come out and do some gigs, I was really looking forward to that."

Beverley Knight reflected: "When I speak of Prince, I still speak of him as though he's here, and even though the physical body is gone, the music is – quite frankly – forever. What I have to say to myself, every time I think of him and feel sad, is: 'But he was *here*, and we managed to enjoy such a huge part of him through his music.' And for me personally, I got to know the man, and I got to touch greatness."

Susannah Melvoin shared something deeply personal about a poignant keepsake. "I just found his waist chain that he would wear on the Parade Tour," she said. "I found it here in my house, among so many other things of his; at the time, thinking, 'I'm so glad I found this.' Then, three weeks later, that horrible emptiness.

"Everyone has processed this differently [among] the people that were very close to him," she went on. "But I can say that for a small group of us, it's a deep, deep, dark well that we're still trying to tap into, to get through. We're going to be doing our best to honor him for all of our time here."

Paul Peterson, her bandmate from The Family, Prince's first signings to Paisley Park, and their twenty-first century incarnation fDeluxe, discussed with me the desperately sad circumstances of his passing. Even they reflected his resolute work ethic, since the addiction to

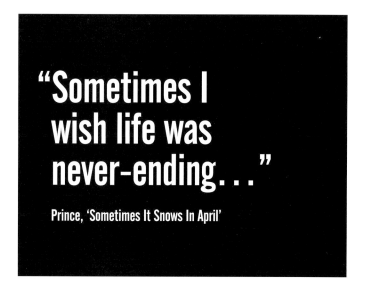

"Sometimes I wish life was never-ending…"

Prince, 'Sometimes It Snows In April'

Left: The MTV Music Video award in the Best Dance Video 1992 for 'Cream'. It is one of four VMA Awards that Prince won in his illustrious career.

Opposite: The Super Bowl half-time show, Febrary 2018.

Above: A still from the Fox sitcom *New Girl*, in which Prince made a cameo appearance in 2014.

Below: Prince in a guitar trade-off with 3RDEYEGIRL during his Hit 'N' Run Tour at Bell Centre on May 23, 2015, in Montreal, Canada. The US funk rock trio of Hannah Welton, Donna Grantis and Ida Kristine Nielsen were Prince's backing band from 2014 until his death in 2016.

part of my musical past that I'm very proud of. I was very lucky to be in his presence during, in my opinion, his most prolific time."

Susan Rogers, his studio familiar in that first heyday (yes, purple patch), added: "I never imagined that one day I would be talking about Prince [in the past tense] at such a relatively young age. I imagined I might be talking about him, and our time together, in my nineties.

"Those of us who knew him well can talk about him, and we can let the public know what kind of a man he was. We are obliged not to canonize him. Prince had his faults, like everyone. We are obliged to tell the truth, but I think the truth is a pretty good story, about a truly great man."

When Prince passed on 21 April 2016, the beautiful closing song of his *Under the Cherry Moon* soundtrack seemed to hang on the breeze as a hauntingly apposite hymn. "Sometimes it snows in April …" he sings eerily. He wishes life was never-ending, but recognizes plaintively that good things never last.

One thing we know: the man who once insisted, with typical outspoken candour, that we call him TAFKAP, still bears that acronym. But now he is the Artist Forever Known as Prince.

painkillers that he hid from even those near to him was borne of his determination that the show must go on.

"It's a tragedy," said Peterson. "I feel so badly that he was in such pain. But I still get calls about him all the time, and it's a wonderful

Top: St. Paul Peterson of The Family, later of fDeluxe, and a solo musician. "I had a much longer tenure with other artists," he says, "but because of the iconic presence that Prince was, and is, I'll always be associated with him. I think that's pretty cool."

Above: Candles lit in remembrance of Prince around his star outside the Warner Theater in Washington, DC. Says Susannah Melvoin: "We're going to be doing our best to honour him for all of our time here".

INDEX

PICTURE CREDITS